EZRA AND NEHEMIAH:
Rebuilding What's Ruined

Iain M. Duguid

New
Growth
Press

newgrowthpress.com

New Growth Press, Greensboro, NC 27401
newgrowthpress.com
Copyright © 2022 by Iain M. Duguid

Cover Design: Faceout Books, faceoutstudio.com
Interior Design and Typesetting: Gretchen Logterman
Exercises and Application Questions: Jack Klumpenhower

ISBN: 978-1-64507-244-7 (Print)
ISBN: 978-1-64507-245-4 (eBook)

Printed in the United States of America

29 28 27 26 25 24 23 22   1 2 3 4 5

Contents

HISTORY OF ISRAEL'S DECLINE AND RESTORATION

ca. 940 BC	King Solomon marries foreign wives who lead him astray, and builds temples to Ammonite and Moabite false gods just outside of Jerusalem (1 Kings 11:1–13).
ca. 930 BC	The kingdom divides into idolatrous Israel in the north with Samaria as its capital city and Judah in the south, where worship of the Lord continues at the temple in Jerusalem but is often corrupted or insincere (1 Kings 12:16–33; Jeremiah 7:1–15).
722 BC	As God's judgment for its rebellion, the Northern Kingdom is destroyed by Assyria and the people assimilated into surrounding cultures. Foreign peoples are relocated into the area around Samaria, where they are taught to claim allegiance to the Lord while still worshiping their false gods as well (2 Kings 17:6–41).
587 BC	Due to its sin, Judah is defeated by Babylon. Jerusalem, with the temple, is turned to rubble. Many of the people are deported into exile in Babylon, where a remnant survives (2 Chronicles 36:15–21).
538 BC	King Cyrus of Persia takes control of the former Babylonian Empire and issues an edict that the people may return to their homeland and rebuild the temple (Ezra 1).
458 BC	Ezra the priest leads a second group of exiles home and initiates spiritual reforms in Jerusalem (Ezra 7).
445 BC	Nehemiah arrives and assumes governorship, rebuilding Jerusalem's walls and enforcing further reforms (Nehemiah 2).

INTRODUCTION

The story of Ezra and Nehemiah plays out against a backdrop of ruins. There's a ruined city, a ruined house of worship, ruined homes—ruined life with God. And as is often the case with the ruined parts of our own lives, the shame is amplified by the fact that the wreckage is largely the people's own fault. They and their ancestors acted foolishly, unfaithfully, godlessly.

And yet, their hope for restoration is in the same God they once spurned: "For he is good, for his steadfast love endures forever" (Ezra 3:11). Their path to a rebuilt city and renewed homes will actually be, at its core, a journey back to God. Such homecomings often involve tears, but there is nothing sweeter. As you study this part of the Bible, you too will be encouraged to return daily to the God who is always faithful to you, and to find rest in him.

This steadfast love of God is most beautifully seen in Jesus, who died for us who were once his enemies to bring us home to himself. So, like the other small group resources in this series, this study guide will repeatedly point you to Christ and that good news. He is the one who brings new life where there is ruin and decay. As Ezra and Nehemiah call to mind challenges and frustrations in your life, you will be reminded to take all those needs to Jesus.

HOW TO USE THIS STUDY

This study guide is designed to help you learn from the Bible within a small group. One theme of Ezra and Nehemiah is

God's people coming together to remember his goodness and to challenge each other to live accordingly. Being in a group helps you believe, repent, and live for God, because these are things Christians do *together*. With this in mind, try to make the group a place where participants can be open about sins, discouragements, and the hard tests of life. Not everyone will be equally quick to share personal struggles—and that's okay—but these lessons will create opportunities for that to happen.

Each participant should have one of these study guides in order to join in reading and be able to work through the exercises during that part of the lesson. There are ten lessons in this study guide. Ezra and Nehemiah combine to make twenty-three chapters of Scripture, so the study will skip some parts of those books (including a few chapters with long lists of names). If you want to read through all of Ezra and Nehemiah, you might decide to read the skipped chapters in between meetings. Other than that, no preparation or homework is required for participants. The study leader, though, should read through both the lesson and the leader's notes in the back of this book before each lesson begins.

Each lesson will take about an hour to complete, perhaps a bit more if your group is large. It will include these elements:

BIG IDEA. This is a summary of the main point of the lesson.

BIBLE CONVERSATION. You will read a passage from the Bible and discuss it. As the heading suggests, the Bible conversation questions are intended to spark a conversation rather than generate correct answers. The leader's notes at the back of this book provide some insights, but don't just turn there for the "right answer." At times you may want to see what the notes say, but always try to answer for yourself first by thinking about the Bible passage.

ARTICLE. This is the main teaching section of the lesson, written by the book's author.

DISCUSSION. The discussion questions following the article will help you apply the teaching to your life.

EXERCISE. The exercise is a section you will complete on your own during group time. You can write in the book if that helps you. You will then share some of what you learned with the group. If the group is large, it may help to split up to share the results of the exercise and to pray, so that everyone has a better opportunity to participate.

WRAP-UP AND PRAYER. Prayer is a critical part of the lesson because your spiritual growth will happen through God's work in you, not by your self-effort. You will be asking him to do that good work.

Rebuilding from the ruins is an often-repeated pursuit as long as we live in this world. Happily, restoration is a specialty for God, who builds holy people from crumbled lives. Be ready for him to do his reconstruction work in you as you come near to him through this study.

Lesson

1

THE LORD'S WORK

BIG IDEA

God stirs up the hearts of his people, and even some who aren't his people, to accomplish his good plans in his perfect time.

BIBLE CONVERSATION *20 MINUTES*

The setup to Ezra and Nehemiah is found in the book of Chronicles, which precedes Ezra and Nehemiah in our Bibles. Chronicles tells how God's people were once united under a godly king, and how they split into the idolatrous Northern Kingdom of Israel and the Southern Kingdom of Judah, where worship of God at the temple in Jerusalem continued but was often corrupted. God judged Israel by allowing it to be conquered and its people assimilated into surrounding cultures, and a century later he disciplined Judah by appointing Babylon to destroy Jerusalem and carry its people into exile. Chronicles ends with the completion of seventy years of exile, as foretold by the prophet Jeremiah,[1] and the decree of King Cyrus of Persia that the exiled people could return home. Ezra-Nehemiah, considered one book in Bible times, tells of the

---

1. Jeremiah 25:8–14

resettlement of Jerusalem. It is structured around three broadly parallel returns from Babylon and Persia.

First return: Ezra 1—6

Year: 538 BC
Leader: Zerubbabel and others
Reconstruction project: Rebuilding the temple

Second return: Ezra 7—10

Year: 458 BC
Leader: Ezra
Reconstruction project: Renewing the Judean community

Third return: Nehemiah 1—7:3

Year: 445 BC
Leader: Nehemiah
Reconstruction project: Restoring the walls of Jerusalem

Celebration: Nehemiah 8—12

The restored community celebrates the completion of the rebuilding work and renews its covenant with the Lord, in accordance with God's law.

Ezra 1 begins with King Cyrus's decree. Cyrus had conquered Babylon and inherited a situation in which many of its residents were exiles from other countries. His solution was to repatriate many to their homelands, placing carefully selected national leaders over them and funding the rebuilding of their national institutions—creating a core of loyal dependents. This probably seemed to Cyrus simply a smart political move, but it was actually the result of God's intervention. The prophets had told of this return, even envisioning an era of tremendous peace and worship.[2] Have someone read **Ezra 1** aloud. Then discuss the questions below:

1. Judging from what details are included in this chapter, what do you think God wants to accomplish in and for his people as he brings them home?

2. Why might it be encouraging for the people to see the same temple-worship items that had been taken from Jerusalem seventy years earlier carefully counted out and returned?

3. When you think about God's work in the world today, what role has he given you: a role like that of the people who personally returned to Jerusalem, the neighbors who stayed behind but supported them, Sheshbazzar who was entrusted with the holy items, or Cyrus? Explain.

****

Now read the following article, written by this study guide's author. Take turns reading it aloud, switching readers at each paragraph break. When you finish, discuss the questions at the end of the article.

---

2. For example, see Isaiah 60—62; Jeremiah 30—31

Lesson

ARTICLE

HOLDING OUT FOR A HERO

5 MINUTES

Many of us, especially those of us who are older, were raised on a "great men" view of history. That is, we understood history to be the story of the exploits of famous men (or, very rarely, a woman) who single-handedly changed the world. Certainly, that is often how we approach Old Testament narratives, searching for the hero whose life story can inspire and instruct us as we model ourselves after him or her.

When it comes to the book of Ezra-Nehemiah, our gaze might fasten on Nehemiah, who fits our culture's vision of a strong and decisive leader. If we did that, however, we would completely miss the point. The book does not focus on Nehemiah as an individual, or even on two individuals, Ezra and Nehemiah. Neither is even present for the first phase of the restoration project, which is the work of many people.

Rather, the book shows us God at work through a variety of leaders and ordinary people, all *partially* accomplishing the restoration of Judah and Jerusalem after the cataclysm of the Babylonian exile. It is a story of God's faithfulness and some forward progress for his people, but it is also a story of the people's relentless struggle to survive in the face of overwhelming opposition.

Each reconstruction effort in Ezra-Nehemiah faces almost constant opposition from neighbors on every side, overcome only with divine help. And the book concludes with an acute awareness of how much remains in ruins in the city of God, closing with an ominous chapter in which all the previous achievements are threatened as soon as Nehemiah is absent from the scene. There is certainly great thankfulness to God for what has been accomplished, but at the same time a constant undercurrent of incompleteness to the fulfillment of God's great promises. A greater work of God will be needed to achieve the fullness of what the prophets promised, which is nothing less than the complete redemption of God's people.

So, this is the book's encouraging message for us: (1) God is faithfully at work in and through us in the messiness of life and ministry in this fallen world, and (2) faithfulness should be celebrated even when so much sin and brokenness continue to be evident in our lives and our churches.

Restoring Jerusalem was not a simple task. The city had been devastated and the temple lay in ruins. The involvement of the entire community was necessary, with those who remained behind in Babylon financially supporting those who returned, helping them to rebuild God's house. Still more important, of course, was the support of the Lord himself. The Lord who had moved the spirit of Cyrus to send the exiles home had to provide the resources necessary for the dangerous journey, and also for the long and challenging task of rebuilding the temple, the city, and the walls of Jerusalem. The book details the Lord's faithfulness in providing for his people through many dangers, toils, and snares.

In one sense, the return of the exiles accomplished frustratingly little. The temple was eventually rebuilt after a twenty-year delay, but those who had seen the first temple thought it disappointing and lacking in glory.[3] And the restored community suffered from much of the same half-heartedness and sin that their ancestors had struggled with—a major theme in the rest of Ezra-Nehemiah.

Yet in another sense, the return was a glorious demonstration of God's faithfulness and forgiveness. Repeatedly in Ezra-Nehemiah, we see the Lord stirring up his people to give and to work, and smoothing out potential obstacles in order to bring his people home from exile and rebuild his city. In the language of Isaiah 40, the God of heaven was lifting up valleys and leveling mountains in order to create a smooth highway for his people to return, making the way ready ultimately for their promised King to come. The unimpressive temple that was finished in Zerubbabel's time, and later renovated and expanded, would one day welcome the Messiah—himself in the surprisingly weak form of a little baby.[4] God's work is not always accomplished in grandeur. Often, his most important acts begin in weakness.

It is in this way that the book speaks most directly into our own lives and churches. We may have visions of accomplishing great things for God and yet find ourselves in frustrating circumstances, making only small progress as we wrestle with difficult people and our own hard hearts. Sometimes God *doesn't* open the doors for us in our attempts to serve him and expand his church. Sometimes we work hard and as faithfully as we can, yet we see very little fruit for our labors. Don't miss what God

---

3. Haggai 2:1–3
4. Luke 2:22–38

is up to in the midst of the chaos. Even in small ways, he is at work in spite of opposition.

Yet the frustrations of the present are not the end of the story. Look forward to the completion of the great work that, through Christ, God has begun in us and around us. He will build his church, and "he who began a good work in you will bring it to completion at the day of Jesus Christ" (Philippians 1:6). Jesus is our "great man" of history. In him, we see God entering into the messiness of life with us—to redeem us and give us a glorious inheritance in him. In his resurrection and ascension, Jesus is the firstfruits of the new creation, the down payment and assurance that God will indeed fulfill everything he has promised. God is faithful and he will do it.

DISCUSSION *10 MINUTES*

What purposes has God accomplished in your life by stirring up the hearts of people around you?

As someone who lives in a later era than the returning exiles (*after* Christ has come, and with his promise that he will return), what greater advantages do you have when you undertake tasks for God?

Lesson

EXERCISE

STIRRED HEARTS

20 MINUTES

A theme in Ezra 1 is how God stirs hearts. He stirs Cyrus to proclaim the restoration of Jerusalem, stirs many to go, and moves others to freely offer support. For this exercise, you will work on your own to consider what God has stirred your heart to do for him and also what frustrations you've felt when God has chosen *not* to stir hearts or remove roadblocks. The exercise will help you think about God's work in your life and also help your group get to know each other.

For each section below, take time on your own to choose a few responses that are true of you. If you can, add a word or two of explanation or detail. When everyone is ready, you'll have a chance to share some of your responses with the rest of the group.

God has stirred my heart to serve him by some way that I . . .

❐ Join his mission to tell others about Jesus: _____.

☑ Show compassion for people in need: homelessness .

☑ Repent of a specific sin: pride, lust .

❐ Serve in the church: _____.

☑ Am faithful in my family or community: _Consistency_ ①

❑ Practice generosity or support others' work: _____.

❑ Draw near to Jesus and grow spiritually: _____.

❑ Am willing to suffer for Jesus: _____.

❑ Use my authority for godly purposes: _____.

☑ Leave what is safe/comfortable, and go out: _____.

☑ Pray for others or for God's work: _friends, brothers, church. guys)_

❑ Other: _____.

I would like to serve God in some way, but I have been frustrated or stalled because God has NOT provided . . .

☑ Stirred up hearts, in me or in others: _motivation, courage_

❑ The giftedness I feel I need: _____.

❑ Certain necessary resources: _____.

❑ Needed support from others: _____.

❑ A clear opportunity or the right church: _____.

☑ A clear direction for getting started: _where to serve_.

❑ An answer to certain objections: _____.

❑ A way through opposition: _____.

☑ Progress against some sin in my life: _selfishness, pride_.

❑ Other: _____.

When the group is ready, explain some of your responses. What has God stirred you to do, and what frustrations remain?

What reasons do you think God might have for sometimes *not* stirring up the hearts of his people, letting roadblocks remain, so that your work for him stalls?

WRAP-UP AND PRAYER *10 MINUTES*

Finish your time together by praying for each other and for the work of the church and its mission. Pray especially that God would both stir hearts and use apparent setbacks to accomplish his purposes.

The next lesson will begin with Ezra 3. If you wish to read through all of Ezra and Nehemiah as a part of your study, you may want to read chapter 2 on your own before the next time your group meets.

Lesson

2

WORSHIP

BIG IDEA

Worship is central to life with God, calling us to look beyond
our present difficulties and to celebrate what Jesus has done
and will do for us.

BIBLE CONVERSATION *20 MINUTES*

Ezra 3 takes place after the returning exiles have arrived in
their homeland. It contains several references to features of
Old Testament worship:

- **The temple** was God's designated place of worship. Both
  the original temple built under King Solomon and its pre-
  decessor, the portable tabernacle, were places for God to be
  among his people, demonstrated by the cloud of his glory
  filling the sanctuary. Both were carefully built according to
  God-given specifications that reflected heavenly worship
  and pointed ahead to Christ.[1]
- **The altar** was a centerpiece of temple worship and was
  necessary for offering sacrifices to the Lord, including burnt offerings acknowledging the people's sin.

---

1. Exodus 26:30; 39:32–43; 40:34–38; 1 Kings 6; 8:10–11; Hebrews 8:5–6

These altar sacrifices could only be offered at the particular temple site God had chosen, on Mount Zion in
Jerusalem.[2]

- **The Feast of Booths** (also called the Feast of Tabernacles
or Shelters) was a yearly gathering during which God's
people lived in makeshift dwellings to commemorate the
exodus, when God brought their ancestors out of Egypt
and they lived in shelters in the wilderness. Special daily
sacrifices on the altar were part of the feast. By the time
of Ezra and Nehemiah, this feast increasingly took on
a forward-looking feel, anticipating the outpouring of
God's Spirit and the nations coming to Jesus.[3]

- **The Levites** were members of the priestly tribe charged
with making sure the temple and its worship were carried out according to God's blueprint. The normal age
for Levites to begin serving was thirty, but twenty-year-
olds serve in Ezra 3, perhaps because most of the returning exiles were young and the number of Levites was
relatively small.[4]

Now have someone read **Ezra 3** aloud, or have a few readers
take turns. Then discuss the questions below:

1. What would you have found exciting about participating
in these events after growing up in exile? Explain.

2. Do you think you would have appreciated or resented the
care taken to follow detailed instructions, "as it is written in
the Law of Moses" (v. 2)? Explain why, and why it matters.

---

2. Leviticus 1; Deuteronomy 12:5–14; 2 Samuel 24:18–25
3. Leviticus 23:42–43; Numbers 29:12–40; Nehemiah 9:20; Zechariah 13—14; John 7:37–39
4. Numbers 4:23, 39; Ezra 2:40–42

3. Do you relate more to those who praised God for the beginnings of worship, or to those who wept over how their worship was still lacking? Explain.

****

Now take turns reading the article aloud, switching readers at each paragraph break. Then discuss the questions at the end of the article.

Lesson

ARTICLE

CELEBRATING THE FEAST

5 MINUTES

As the first wave of Jews returned, their initial need was to go to their hometowns and build some kind of temporary accommodation for themselves, which would have scattered them throughout Judah. But they all promptly regathered as one man to go up to Jerusalem and celebrate the Feast of Shelters.

The feast reminded them of the wilderness wanderings of their forefathers and the Lord's provision of the promised land. Yet these particular Jews had themselves experienced a kind of second exodus, this time from Babylon, and they were once again receiving a part of the land as God's renewed gift to them. For them, the feast was not a recollection of ancient history, but a poignant celebration of the Lord's present goodness and an anticipation of greater things to come. Living in temporary shelters while inhabiting the land was an annual reminder that God's promise was always much more than a real-estate deal. The land of Canaan was a shadow of the true and heavenly promised land that the Lord had prepared for his people.

The feast stimulated the people to participate in communal rebuilding activities—first the altar, and then the temple. The ceremony to celebrate the foundation of the new temple recalled the days of old, with priests and Levites in their sacred robes with their instruments, just as David had directed. The choirs seem to have sung responsively, adapting the refrain from Psalm 136, "For his steadfast love endures forever," to, "For his steadfast love endures forever *toward Israel*" (Ezra 3:11). The people were not merely celebrating God's general goodness to humanity, but specifically his faithfulness to his covenant people. He was bringing them back from exile and restoring them to their land.

Yet in the midst of the unity of this scene, the first note of discord emerges. Not everyone wept for joy. Some older members of the crowd cried out with sorrow over the relative lack of glory of the new building. It wasn't like the one Solomon had built: it lacked the gold and silver and, more importantly, it did not witness the visible outpouring of the divine glory upon it in the way the tabernacle and Solomon's temple had.

This story captures the excitement and the challenge of beginning a new work for God. There are rarely enough people and resources to meet the needs, and threats abound on all sides. But the people began with exactly the right focus, gathering for worship. They also understood the centrality of sacrifice to their religion: as sinful men and women, a ransom needed to be paid to atone for them and enable them to stand in the presence of a holy God. The blood of bulls and goats did not in itself accomplish that cleansing, but it pointed them forward to the gospel—how God himself would provide a lamb to take away the sins of the world.

What is more, the temple was not merely a place of sacrifice, but a house of prayer and praise.[5] The praise of God is, after all,

---

5. 1 Kings 8; Isaiah 56:7

our chief end as men and women—what we were made for. So the priests and the Levites led the people in worship, directing their gaze back to the Lord's *hesed*, his steadfast and faithful love for his people.

The feast was the ideal time for the Israelites to be summoned to look both backward and forward. As they camped out, they would remember the wilderness wanderings that were the bitter fruit of the rebellion of that generation, and also the final conquest of the land. These were powerful lessons of God's grace as this new generation returned from the exile, itself the bitter fruit of many generations of rebellion. But the feast also invited them to look forward to the final victory and enthronement of their God on the day when all nations would bring their sacrifices and praises to Mount Zion.[6]

We often live our lives captured by the present, whether absorbed by its successes or overwhelmed by its disasters and tragedies. Worship calls our eyes away from ourselves and our efforts and invites us to look back and look forward. We look back to Christ's first coming, with glory veiled in the humility of a servant's form. At the cross, he didn't look like the triumphant king; he seemed a man under a curse. But that curse was for us, as Jesus offered himself as the Lamb of God, presenting his own blood on the heavenly altar. In his death, he fulfilled everything the temple sacrifices represented.

Today Christ is no longer on the cross. He has ascended on high. As we worship, we look forward to his coming again in glory when he will lead his brothers in singing the Lord's praises in the congregation.[7] Christ's resurrection and ascension are

---

6. Isaiah 2:2–4
7. Hebrews 2:12 (quoting Psalm 22:22)

the ultimate display of the Lord's *hesed* to the true Israel, a song that one day we too will sing in glory.

In the meantime, this perspective helps us in the muck and mire of life in a fallen world. It is hard to build God's kingdom, whether in our own hearts, in our families, in the local church, or as we take the gospel to the world. The opposition is great, and the progress often seems meager in comparison to stories we have heard from church history. No matter: God is building his kingdom. His final glory is assured, and in him so is ours. Our life here on earth is merely the front porch of our eternal home, where even now our inheritance is safely stored up in him.

DISCUSSION *10 MINUTES*

Why might it be especially important to worship God when you *aren't* "feeling it," or when it seems God is making little progress in your life? *First things first.*

Tell about a time when present-day troubles or successes consumed you, so that you failed to see what Jesus has done for you and will do when he returns.

"Every good endeavor" By Tim Keller

– sufficiency w/ or w/o proficiency

– not being enough

– business

– how do you motivate yourself @ work?
– frame as loving others

Lesson

EXERCISE

LOOK BACK, LOOK AHEAD

20 MINUTES

The Bible says a Christian worship service is much more than a useful spiritual pick-me-up chosen for its pleasing songs and helpful pep talks. Rather, the Bible views our assemblies as events of cosmic significance that exceed those of Ezra-Nehemiah in glory: "You have come to Mount Zion and to the city of the living God, the heavenly Jerusalem, and to innumerable angels in festal gathering, and to the assembly of the firstborn who are enrolled in heaven, and to God, the judge of all, and to the spirits of the righteous made perfect, and to Jesus, the mediator of a new covenant" (Hebrews 12:22–24).

You will better appreciate worship when you, like the people in Ezra 3, look not only at today but also look back and look forward as you worship. For this exercise, work on your own to see how you might do that. Read the descriptions that go with each element of Christian worship listed below. For each item, ask yourself if it is something you realize and treasure about worship.

If you currently sense and appreciate that this is happening when you worship, you might mark it with a CHECKMARK.

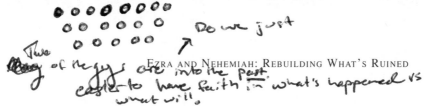

(handwritten notes in top margin) Do we just ↗ / The Body of Christ are into the past / easier to have faith in what's happened vs / what will.

If you would like to become more aware and appreciative of this when you worship, you might mark it with an UPWARD ARROW.

Pick one item in each list that most makes you want to sing, pray, hear God's Word, etc. You might mark it with a STAR.

When we gather to SING TOGETHER . . .

_____ **We look back.** Our singing joins with the great assemblies of God's people who have come before us in praising God for all he has done. "Sing to him, sing praises to him; tell of all his wondrous works!" (Psalm 105:2).

_____ **We look at Jesus today.** Our brother Jesus is spiritually with us and sings along with us when we worship—as he will when he returns. "[Jesus] is not ashamed to call them brothers, saying, 'I will tell of your name to my brothers; in the midst of the congregation I will sing your praise'" (Hebrews 2:11–12).

_____ **We look ahead.** We anticipate our grand destiny, the day Jesus will raise us from our graves and we will join the heavenly singing of all nations around the Lord's throne. "Your dead shall live; their bodies shall rise. You who dwell in the dust, awake and sing for joy!" (Isaiah 26:19).

When we gather to PRAY TOGETHER . . .

_____ **We look back.** We pray with the certainty that God loves to say yes to his people and will give us all that is good, having already given us Jesus. "He who did not spare his own Son but gave him up for us all, how will he not also with him graciously give us all things?" (Romans 8:32).

_____ **We look at Jesus today.** We come before our Father with utmost confidence, knowing that at the same moment Jesus is praying with us and for us in heaven. "He is able to save to the uttermost those who draw near to God through him, since he always lives to make intercession for them" (Hebrews 7:25).

_____ **We look ahead.** We pray for Jesus to return soon and defeat evil forever, knowing that such prayers surely are heard in heaven and will be made true on earth. "The smoke of the incense, with the prayers of the saints, rose before God from the hand of the angel. Then the angel took the censer and filled it with fire from the altar and threw it on the earth" (Revelation 8:4–5).

When we gather to HEAR GOD'S WORD PREACHED AND READ TO US . . .

_____ **We look back.** We see how God's Word has sustained his people in times past, and we are eager to be fed by that same Word—which is even more vivid now that Jesus has come. "Long ago, at many times and in many ways, God spoke to our fathers by the prophets, but in these last days he has spoken to us by his Son" (Hebrews 1:1–2).

_____ **We look at Jesus today.** We hunger for God's Word because we realize that we live and grow by it, as Jesus prayed for us: "Sanctify them in the truth; your word is truth" (John 17:17).

_____ **We look ahead.** We understand that our only hope of resurrection lies in the power of God's Word over every part of our being, and we want to taste the power of his voice already today. "An hour is coming when all who are in the tombs will hear his voice and come out" (John 5:28–29).

When we gather to GIVE OFFERINGS TOGETHER . . .

_____ **We look back.** We remember all that Jesus has done for us and we respond with gratitude. "For you know the grace of our Lord Jesus Christ, that though he was rich, yet for your sake he became poor, so that you by his poverty might become rich" (2 Corinthians 8:9).

_____ **We look at Jesus today.** What an honor it is to support the church's work in this exciting era, a time when Jesus is proclaimed to all nations and our love for others is a worldwide witness that brings him praise! "You will be enriched in every way to be generous in every way, which through us will produce thanksgiving to God" (2 Corinthians 9:11).

_____ **We look ahead.** We act on the truth that earthly treasures will not last but heavenly investments are forever. "[The rich] are to do good, to be rich in good works, to be generous and ready to share, thus storing up treasure for themselves as a good foundation for the future, so that they may take hold of that which is truly life" (1 Timothy 6:18–19).

When we gather to CELEBRATE THE LORD'S SUPPER TOGETHER . . .

_____ **We look back.** We remember and believe that Jesus's death has fully paid for all our sins. "For as often as you eat this bread and drink the cup, you proclaim the Lord's death until he comes" (1 Corinthians 11:26).

We look at Jesus today. We take places of honor at the table of the world's greatest King, who richly provides all we need. "Jesus said to them, 'I am the bread of life; whoever comes to me shall not hunger, and whoever believes in me shall never thirst'" (John 6:35).

We look ahead. We whet our appetites for the heavenly marriage supper of the Lamb, when we will celebrate being with Jesus forever. "I tell you I will not drink again of this fruit of the vine until that day when I drink it new with you in my Father's kingdom" (Matthew 26:29).

When the group is ready, share some of your responses. Which of these truths about worship was new to you? How do you already look back and look ahead when you worship, and what truths about worship do you want to treasure more?

Do you notice any patterns in what parts of Christ's work (past, present, future) most hold your attention?

What part of looking back or looking ahead most encourages you to work at building God's kingdom, and why?

WRAP-UP AND PRAYER *10 MINUTES*

Include prayers for worship in your closing time together. Pray for God to enlarge your appreciation for worship, and pray for those who lead the worship services you attend.

Lesson

3

FACING OPPOSITION

BIG IDEA

The Christian life often brings opposition and then discouragement, but King Jesus uses even apparent setbacks for his glory and our good.

BIBLE CONVERSATION *20 MINUTES*

Ezra 4 is about persecution, and it is not merely the story of a single experience of persecution but rather the account of a lifetime (and more) of constant opposition to God's work.

- Verses 1–5 tell of opposition the returning exiles faced soon after beginning their rebuilding projects authorized by King Cyrus.
- Verse 6 jumps ahead in time to mention a similar struggle during the reign of a later Persian emperor, Ahasuerus.
- Verses 7–23 look even further ahead to later rebuilding projects, recounting how the opposition continued into the reign of Artaxerxes, about a century after it began.

The result is a chapter that breaks from a strict chronological telling of the story to describe a hundred years of threats, subversions, slanders, and defeats for those whose hearts were set on rebuilding the temple and the city of Jerusalem. The author will return to the main storyline in chapters 5 and 6 to report that halted work on the temple began again, but even then there will be more interference and delays before the project is finished and the temple dedicated.

Here in chapter 4, the conflict begins with an apparent offer of help from neighbors already living in the area. These people presented themselves as fellow worshipers of the Lord, but were foreigners who had been resettled in the land following the Assyrian conquest of the Northern Kingdom of Israel. They had been taught about the Lord by a priest from that religiously-confused kingdom, so it is not surprising that although they claimed to fear the Lord, they "also served their own gods, after the manner of the nations from among whom they had been carried away" (2 Kings 17:33).

Have someone read **Ezra 4:1—5:2** aloud, or have several readers take turns. Then discuss the questions below:

1.   Refusing the initial offer of help led to a hundred years of opposition. Why was it still right to refuse that offer?

2.   What tactics are used in the letter the adversaries sent to the king? Are the tactics fair? Do they feel familiar? Explain.

3.   Verse 4 says the opposition made the people discouraged and afraid. What happenings in this chapter would be discouraging or scary to you, and why?

****

Now read the article aloud, taking turns by paragraph, and then discuss the questions that follow.

Lesson

ARTICLE

ENDURING PERSECUTION

5 MINUTES

The author of Ezra-Nehemiah has gathered together the events of chapter 4 to highlight a reality Paul describes in 2 Timothy 3:12. "All who desire to live a godly life in Christ Jesus will be persecuted." The community of returning exiles represented no danger to their neighbors. They had no expansionist goals or saber-rattling military. All they wanted was to be allowed to live in peace, but this was precisely what their neighbors would not allow to happen.

Having failed to infiltrate the work, the enemies of God's people set themselves to oppose the work. They could not invade Judah and stop the building effort, so they sought to discourage the Jews through intimidation and by raising diplomatic obstacles in the Persian court—a tactic they continued through most of the next century. A classic example of this deceptive diplomacy is the letter sent during the reign of Artaxerxes, which paints God's people as dangerous rebels.

For those who know biblical history, there's rich irony in this letter. Jerusalem had indeed been a rebellious city for centuries—not only against the Assyrians and Babylonians, but more profoundly against the Lord, their true King. That rebellion against the Lord was the real reason the city had been laid waste by the Babylonians.[1] Now, those who had returned were trying to turn over a new leaf, becoming obedient to the great King. This actually made them more faithful citizens of their earthly overlords, the Persians. So, the charge against Jerusalem was true in a sense, but out of date. God had made them new people. He was reestablishing them as a new and faithful community, with their hearts purged of their former rebelliousness.

However, the letter apparently convinced the king, and he ordered the work in Jerusalem to be stopped. Opposition is a regular part of every Christian's life and every fruitful ministry and church. As Paul reminds us in Acts 14:22, "through many tribulations we must enter the kingdom of God." Trials and opposition can be deeply discouraging for all of us and may lead to us giving up the work, at least for a season. In those situations, there are several things we should remember.

First, opposition and trials are normal. A century or more of opposition taught Ezra and Nehemiah that truth. We too should not be surprised by opposition—especially in the New Testament era, where we see clearly that we follow a rejected and crucified Messiah. If our master Jesus faced opposition, why should we expect anything different?

Sometimes civil authorities will aid and protect Christians, while at other times they will obstruct and persecute them. But our great King remains on the throne. Sometimes he opens doors for his servants, while at other times he closes down a church or a ministry that seemed vibrant in presenting the gospel. This same God chose to have his best church planter,

---

1. 2 Chronicles 36:12–21

the apostle Paul, spend years in Roman prison cells rather than out sharing the gospel. The fruit of that divine plan was the encouragement of other believers to be bold,[2] plus the writing of a significant part of the New Testament, but it must have been puzzling for the Christians of Paul's day.

Second, believers may have to battle discouragement. When hopes are disappointed and life is hard, it is easy to slip into discouragement and fear. Yet if we really believe that the Lord is sovereign and will work all things together for good, why should we be disheartened and afraid? If we die, we go to be with him. If we live, then we may serve him in whatever ways he allows us to do so. We may perhaps serve in a "day of small things," as Zechariah 4:10 describes the Ezra-Nehemiah era. But we serve the God whose kingdom is like the mustard seed, which grows from tiny beginnings into a large tree. We may not see the fruits of our labors during our lives, but if we labor in the Lord, we know that our labor is not in vain.

Third, our opponents cannot win. The century of opposition delayed but did not prevent the rebuilding of the altar, temple, and walls of Jerusalem. The Lord always gets his way, and his purposes always triumph in the end. Nowhere is this principle clearer than in the life of Jesus. He faced powerful opposition, not just from the nations but from his own people. They conspired to put him to death, and seemed to have succeeded in their wicked designs. Yet this merely accomplished God's perfect plan to redeem a people for himself. This should give us great boldness to proclaim the gospel in the face of the greatest opposition or the most challenging circumstances. God is still God, and when we are at our weakest and most helpless, his glory shines all the more clearly.

---

2. Philippians 1:12–14

Finally, God's Word can strengthen and stir our spirits for the fight. At the end of our passage, God uses the arrival of Haggai and Zechariah to encourage and challenge his people out of discouragement. God's word, applied by God's Spirit, stirred the hearts of his people to want to serve him again, whatever the opposition. This is typically the way real change happens in us and in our communities: God's Word is applied by his Spirit to bring deep-seated transformation.

DISCUSSION *10 MINUTES*

How have you, or churches you have been in, faced opposition in doing the Lord's work? How frustrated have you felt?

The article mentions several comforts to remember during times of opposition. Which of them have you found helpful, and what other comforts has Jesus given you?

EXERCISE

DEALING WITH DISCOURAGEMENT

20 MINUTES

Discouragement is a common response to the opposition a Christian life brings you. To complete this exercise, you'll decide how you've been discouraged, look at a Bible passage that addresses that discouragement, and then report back to the group on what you found in the Bible. Many of the Bible passages selected for this exercise are psalms, which are the Bible's prayers. Prayer is a basic first response to discouragement, and a way to practice faith. When you pray, you take the burdens of opposition off of yourself and place them on God, who can handle every difficulty.

Pick <u>one</u> item from the list below that reflects a discouraged way you tend to respond to opposition in your Christian life. Read the brief gospel answer that goes with it, and then read the Bible passage that addresses it. Note some things the Bible says that you find helpful or eye-opening. You'll share those things with the group later.

Discouraged way I respond to opposition: "I can't beat this. Too much is against me."

The gospel says: Jesus can overcome it. Nothing will stand against him.

READ: Psalm 3

Discouraged way I respond to opposition: "I *must* beat this. God is counting on me."

The gospel says: Your responsibility—and your comfort—is to count on God.

READ: Psalm 62

Discouraged way I respond to opposition: "This shouldn't happen to me when I'm serving God!"

The gospel says: Suffering is expected and connects you to Jesus and his glory.

READ: 1 Peter 4:12–19

Discouraged way I respond to opposition: "There's no end in sight. I'm ready to quit."

The gospel says: Jesus knows it's hard to live for him, but he has promised to give you all you need and to lead you to joy.

READ: John 16:20–24

Discouraged way I respond to opposition: "This must be all my fault. Something is wrong with me."

The gospel says: Oppression often means that you're doing what's *right*, and that God loves you dearly.

READ: Hebrews 12:1–11

Discouraged way I respond to opposition: "God has left me all alone in this."

The gospel says: Jesus has promised to be with you always, and he may actually feel closer if you look to him in your struggle.

READ: Psalm 43

Discouraged way I respond to opposition: "No good can come out of this for me."

The gospel says: God loves you and works everything—even opposition and setbacks—for your good, to fit you to live with him.

READ: Deuteronomy 8:1–10

Discouraged way I respond to opposition: "My own sin has messed this up, so there's no hope."

The gospel says: Yes, your sin is bad. But in Jesus, you have both the Spirit's power to start overcoming your sin and complete forgiveness no matter how much you still fail.

READ: Psalm 25

Notes on the Bible passage you read:

When the group is ready, tell which response you chose and why. Also share some parts of the Bible passage you read that you find helpful.

What part of the passage you read might become a prayer for you, and why would that prayer help you when you face opposition?

WRAP-UP AND PRAYER *10 MINUTES*

Take time now to bring some of the prayers from the exercise before your Father.

The next lesson will be on Ezra 7. If you are reading through all of Ezra-Nehemiah, you might want to read Ezra 5 and 6 on your own before the next meeting.

Handwritten notes at top of page:
- Russian Nesting Dolls
- All Exiles
- Alienation from body, home

Switch to 1st person

4

DEVOTION TO GOD

BIG IDEA

A right commitment to obeying God should not be a burden to earn our own righteousness, nor a license to obey only when we feel like it, but a love for God's commands that flows from Jesus's love for us.

BIBLE CONVERSATION *20 MINUTES*

Ezra 7 begins the account of the second return from exile, about eighty years after the first. By this point, the first phase of reconstruction had been completed. In spite of stop-and-start progress, the temple in Jerusalem was rebuilt. The house of God was rededicated with joy. The people celebrated the Passover together, committing themselves to a life of purity separate from the peoples of the land—though anyone who gave up their idols could join the community of God: "It was eaten by the people of Israel who had returned from exile, and also by everyone who had joined them and separated himself from the uncleanness of the peoples of the land to worship the LORD, the God of Israel" (6:21).

It was now time for phase 2 of reconstruction: rebuilding the community of God's people around a shared commitment to the law of God. The leading figure in this project would be a priest named Ezra. Have someone read **Ezra 7** aloud, or have several readers take turns. Then discuss the questions below:

1. What do you notice about Ezra that makes him highly qualified to lead God's people, and why are these characteristics important in a godly leader?
    Son of AARON

2. Artaxerxes was a pagan king, but what do you find admirable about his approach to the true God? What do you find troubling or not quite right?

3. In the last verse of the chapter, Ezra says he was encouraged. What about these events would encourage you, and why?

****

Next, read the article aloud. Switch readers at each paragraph break. Then discuss the questions that follow.

LOVING GOD'S LAW

5 MINUTES

In chapter 7 we first meet Ezra, who is introduced as a priest and a scribe. He has an impressive genealogy tracing back to Aaron, the first high priest, and *scribe* denotes a class of priests who were experts in the law of Moses. After seventy years of exile, many Israelites would have had a hazy understanding of the law. The vast majority did not own a Torah scroll, and many might not have been able to read.

The need of the hour was for an expert well-versed in all of the law's statutes and rules—the detailed outworking of its principles—to instruct the people in the way they should go. After all, failure to keep the terms of the Mosaic covenant brought God's people into exile in the first place. Ezra was commissioned to instruct the people, and even given the authority to discipline those who might disobey the law. A shared commitment to God's law would provide the people with a common foundation on which to rebuild their fractured community.

Yet for some Christians today, Ezra's mission might seem very alien. Teaching people to obey the commands of the God of heaven, with all of its many rules, may sound like a legalistic enterprise—the exact opposite of preaching the gospel! But this misunderstands both the law and the gospel. God's commandments are "holy and righteous and good" (Romans 7:12). Legalism is not a problem with God's commands but a problem with us. We too easily misuse God's commands, trying to build a résumé of righteousness to justify ourselves and feed our pride. Or we make the opposite error, rejecting God's commands in favor of what feels right to us—perhaps under the label of "grace." Neither is a Christian approach to God's commands.

Ezra's mission was not simply to teach the law, as if he thought that with a little more effort the returned exiles could live up to God's perfect standard. That *would* have been legalism. But Ezra was also commissioned to buy bulls, rams, and lambs for the altar of the temple in Jerusalem. These sacrifices prescribed by the law of Moses were a constant reminder that even with their best efforts, the Jewish community could never attain to God's holiness. The sacrifices reminded them and us that our only hope rests in Christ's righteousness, which fulfilled the law perfectly in our place, and in his death as our spotless substitute.

At the same time, the free gift of Christ's righteousness should not make us lawless. Rather, God's grace frees us from serving our own desires so that we desire to please God by doing what he tells us. A life of meditation on God's law is, after all, the pathway to human flourishing (see Psalm 1). As the Heidelberg Catechism reminds us, the *grace* of God that is the answer to human *guilt* teaches us to live obedient lives of deep *gratitude*.[1]

Notice that Artaxerxes had a legalist's approach to God. As a polytheist, he feared the power of the many national gods worshiped in his empire. By providing resources to maintain the worship of "the God of heaven" in Jerusalem, he hoped to

---

1. For example, see the catechism's question and answer 2 and 86.

avert the potential for the wrath of that deity to curse him and his sons (v. 23). Presumably, he also hoped Israel's deity would be pleased with his gifts and his efforts to ensure that the God of heaven's worship was properly carried out, and would use whatever powers he might possess for Artaxerxes's good. He was trying to earn God's favor.

In contrast, Ezra's desire to obey and worship God flowed from a deep awareness of how God had already been good to his people. Ezra had no doubt where the credit for the king's favor lay. He blessed the Lord, the God of his ancestors, to whom the Lord had promised the land, thanking him for his provision (v. 27). It was the Lord who motivated Artaxerxes to beautify the temple that God's people had rebuilt with such difficulty,[2] and it was the Lord who had showed Ezra his *hesed*, his covenant faithfulness, in giving the favor of a pagan king and his advisors. The result of such evident favor of God at the outset of his mission heartened Ezra for the difficult and dangerous journey back to Judah that lay ahead of him.

In chapter 8, Ezra will employ all his diplomatic skill to recruit Levites and temple servants for the trip. But this too, Ezra will attribute to "the good hand of our God" (8:18). And despite traveling rough roads beset with bandits and robbers, while carrying significant quantities of gold and silver, Ezra will decide not to ask the king for an armed escort, since he had told the king that the Lord would protect them against their enemies (8:22). Instead, the travelers will fast and pray for safety, and the Lord will answer their prayers. Ezra was a man of faith.

We may not all share Ezra's calling to return his society to biblical values (with the complete support of an unbelieving

---

2. See Isaiah 60:7

government!), but we are faced with many difficult challenges as we pursue righteousness in our churches, our families, our communities, or at work. Ezra models for us a remarkable blend of political awareness, diplomatic skill, and leadership that is bathed in prayer and thankful dependence on God. Yet even Ezra's skills and faith would not transform post-exilic Judah completely. Jesus Christ is the only one able to give us the new hearts and new spirits we need if we are indeed to come to love God's commands, as Ezra did—not as our means of redemption, but as our guide for living lives of thankful holiness in God's world.

DISCUSSION *10 MINUTES*

Which of God's commands most easily becomes a source of pride for you? Or which most easily becomes a way you feel you must perform to earn your salvation?

Which of God's commands do you most easily neglect? Which does your culture neglect?

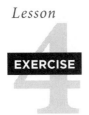

THREE APPROACHES TO GOD'S COMMANDS

20 MINUTES

The article mentioned three different approaches you might take toward God's commands:

1. You might **feel burdened** by God's commands, trying to appease or earn points with God like Artaxerxes.
2. You might **sidestep** God's commands, preferring to decide for yourself what is best, even if you call it living for God.
3. You might **love** God's commands like Ezra.

The third approach, love for God's commands, is the one that flows from the gospel—from the joy and confidence and power of knowing Jesus as your Savior. But even if that is true of you, there will be times your approach is more like the first two, since you are still growing in the gospel.

For this exercise, a series of questions will prompt you to think about your approach to God's commands. Work on your own to answer each question as honestly as you can, noting or circling all the numbered responses that fit you. For each question, try to pick at least one response that comes closest, even if you realize it isn't the gospel response. When everyone is done, you'll discuss your results.

What is your gut response to Ezra's appointment to teach and enforce God's laws?

1. Ezra's ministry makes me think, "It's about time those people shape up" or, "They're going to be in trouble!"
2. Ezra's task feels harsh, authoritarian, or otherwise wrong.
3. Ezra's ministry makes me think, "God is being so good to his people by giving them a teacher who loves his law."

How do you respond to discussions or teaching about how to obey God?

1. Such teaching often makes me feel superior to others, guilty when compared to others, or on-the-spot to perform better.
2. Such teaching feels unhealthy if there's too much of it, or it feels like it might uncomfortably disrupt a life that's already working for me.
3. Such teaching is part of God's work in my life to make me more like Jesus and, when I do sin, to show me how much I need Jesus and coax me closer to him.

How do you respond to discussions or teaching about sin?

1. Talk about sin makes me (1) feel condemned, (2) reassure myself I'm doing okay because I have the worst sins under control, or (3) pick some outward sins to fix so I can prove to God I'm really trying.
2. I dismiss talk about sin as too accusatory, or as something I don't need to be very concerned about since Jesus died for me and God is all about grace.

3. Talk about sin helps me fight it confidently alongside Jesus, who alone defeats sin. He has fully rescued me from sin's penalty, freed me from sin's power so that I can resist it, and one day will eradicate sin from me and the world forever.

How do you think about your relationship with God?

1. When I think about God, I wonder what I can do to make him think better of me.
2. I know God is *supposed* to be my delight, but other joys and affirmations in my life feel more satisfying.
3. I think of God's unchanging, fatherly love. He counts me completely forgiven in Christ so that I don't need to pretend to be better than I am, but learn to depend on him more and more each day.

What is your approach to a life of loving others?

1. Often, my "love for others" is really self-interest. I act loving to feel better about myself or to impress God or others.
2. My "love for others" is usually limited to what I enjoy doing anyway.
3. My love for others flows from Jesus's eternal love for me. Freed from both the pressure to perform and the lure of this world's lesser pleasures, I can lay down my life to truly love others.

What is your approach to the work of the church and its mission?

1. I get involved in the Lord's work hoping to earn the approval of God or others, or to feel better about myself or my commitment level.

2. Getting involved in the Lord's work, or supporting it, feels like it should be totally optional. It's important I not feel pressured if I don't feel the calling.

3. My involvement in the Lord's work flows from my excitement about Jesus: gratitude that he has made me God's child, eagerness to learn to be like him, and confidence that he is calling people to faith and reclaiming his world.

When the group is ready, share some of your responses. Did any patterns emerge, such as a tendency toward #1 (feeling burdened) or #2 (sidestepping) responses?

How has God been growing you in #3 (gospel) responses, and how can you grow further?

What truths about Jesus, if you more deeply believed and enjoyed them, might help you approach God's commands in a more gospel-centered way? Explain.

WRAP-UP AND PRAYER *10 MINUTES*

Pray for your growth in the gospel, for freedom from the burden of trying to earn your righteousness or feed your pride, and for the power and desire to obey God.

The next lesson will begin with Ezra 9. If you are reading through all of Ezra-Nehemiah, you might want to read Ezra 8 on your own before the next meeting.

Lesson

5

LAMENT OVER SIN

BIG IDEA

Confession and humble lament are righteous reactions to sin, and they encourage us in key matters of holy living, such as having godly marriages.

BIBLE CONVERSATION *20 MINUTES*

Chapters 9 and 10 of Ezra concern intermarriage with people who worship idols. In some translations, the Israelites are labelled a "holy race" (more literally, "holy seed"). But the issue is not inter*racial* marriage as we understand it, since the foreign people they are forbidden to marry were ethnically related to the Israelites, and since any foreigners who gave up their idols were welcome to join the community. Rather, the problem is *religious* defilement. Five of the nations mentioned represent the evil inhabitants of the promised land whom Israel was supposed to drive out in the days of Joshua, and the others are nations who had a particularly destructive history with Israel. How could Israel be "a light for the nations" (Isaiah 49:6) and produce "godly offspring/seed" (Malachi 2:15) from unholy unions with unbelievers?

Also, intermarriage in the ancient world was usually about forming alliances. The people of Israel were few in number and poor, and it made sense (from a worldly perspective) to enhance their fortunes by marrying foreign women. King Solomon had used this same reasoning centuries before when he established a huge harem of foreign wives, with devastating results that propelled the people toward idolatry.[1] So, the women and children involved were likely being used for personal gain rather than being in a proper, caring marriage. This may be another reason Ezra is quick to agree that these wives should be "put away," again with the emphasis on the religious purity of the congregation (10:8). We can assume this did not mean total abandonment of those women, as the passage points out that Ezra followed the law of Moses which has many provisions for compassion.

With this background in mind, have some volunteers take turns reading **Ezra 9:1—10:17**, which begins with a report Ezra receives upon arriving in Jerusalem with the second group of returning exiles. Then discuss the questions below:

1. As a godly leader, what does Ezra do in this passage that you find especially admirable or worth copying? Explain.

2. Consider the results of Ezra's heartfelt and visible confession. How do those results compare to what you've seen happen in similar situations when people openly lament and confess sin?

****

Now take turns by paragraph reading the article aloud. When you finish, discuss the questions at the end of the article.

---

1. 1 Kings 11

A GODLY LEADER

5 MINUTES

Ezra's humble dependence upon God was on striking display in chapter 8. Facing a difficult and dangerous journey, he had led those who were with him in fasting, humbling themselves before God, and seeking his blessing. So when Ezra arrived in Jerusalem, it must have been devastating for him to discover the extent of the compromise that was going on. Many people, even priests and Levites, had not kept themselves separate from the surrounding nations but had intermarried with them.

Artaxerxes had invested Ezra with the legal power to punish transgressors of God's law with fines, imprisonment, or even death. Yet Ezra's immediate response was not to discipline the guilty and hand out heavy punishments, but to lament his people's unfaithfulness to God. He tore his garments, pulled out hair from his head and beard as a sign of mourning, and sat on the ground appalled.

Ezra's primary role among the people was to be their priest. This included teaching the people the law of God, but it also involved interceding for them in prayer. At the time of the evening sacrifice, Ezra got up and addressed God rather than the people. He did not act like a righteous outsider condemning the people, but lamented "our iniquities" and "our guilt."

These societal sins shamed *him* too, even though he was not personally guilty.

Ezra confessed that, by intermarrying, the people were flouting God's word given to them by Moses and reiterated by the prophets. The logical outcome of their sin should be that this time the Lord would wipe out his people completely, with no remnant remaining alive. After all that God had done for them and the way they had consistently abused his grace, God would have been perfectly just if he had followed that course of action.

But God provided a happier outcome: the repentance of his people. Although Ezra did not directly tell the people to put away their foreign wives, his prayer had an immediate impact on those around him. A large crowd joined him in his penitence, weeping bitterly. One of the leaders stepped forward and proposed making a covenant to put away the foreign wives and their children, according to the law. In response to Ezra's whole-hearted lament, the people rose up and encouraged him, and soon they took action. He did not have to wield his punitive authority. He won people over by his godly humility and distress.

Some people think all Christians are angry and self-righteous, but it would be hard to believe that about Ezra. Sin breaks Ezra's heart. He identifies himself as a fellow sinner in community with those around him, rather than preaching to them from a position of moral superiority.

At the same time, Ezra doesn't treat sin lightly. He understands that the people's unfaithfulness threatened the very existence of the remnant who had returned, because God is not only loving and compassionate but also just and holy. And in his people, God was preserving a distinct lineage with a holy calling that would give rise to the Messiah. It would not do for God's people to disregard that lineage and lose their distinctiveness, nor brush aside their sin.

The issue of intermarriage with people who do not share our faith remains important (and pastorally challenging) in our own time. We often think of the difficulties it causes for the believing partner in trying to maintain their faith commitment, which are real and substantial. Yet the passages about intermarriage in the post-exilic era (Ezra 9, Nehemiah 13, and Malachi 2) are more concerned about the issue of godly offspring.

Marriage is not simply a means of pleasing ourselves by finding a suitable companion, or (in Ezra's context) cementing business and political relationships to gain more power and wealth. Marriage is also, if God wills, a means of extending the kingdom by having and discipling children. The Bible sets before us the vision of raising godly offspring for the sake of God's kingdom. Even those who are unable to have physical children of their own may pursue the mandate for godly offspring through adoption, or by investing spiritually in the lives of the children of others. There are many young people in our world who are functionally orphans, even while both parents still live, in desperate need of people willing to heed God's call to be spiritual parents.

Ezra's prayer was incomplete. He did not ask for mercy or forgiveness from the Lord. But his prayer still presupposes the fact that God is a merciful and forgiving God. At the same time, God's forgiveness doesn't leave us free to cohabit comfortably with our sin. We need to face up to our sin and deal with it.

Ultimately, God faced up to our sin and dealt with it by sending the holy seed promised to Adam and Eve, Jesus Christ.[2] Jesus

2. Genesis 3:15

came and inhabited our world without taint or compromise, yet he died the death we deserve because of our repeated compromises with our many sins. In this way, God creates for himself a holy people, united to his Son and separate from the lost world around us. This is the good news of salvation for deeply broken sinners that we are called upon to shout from the rooftops in the midst of our own very mixed-up communities.

DISCUSSION *10 MINUTES*

What challenges do you and the church today face when it comes to having godly marriages that produce godly offspring? What does Ezra teach you about facing those challenges?

What role does lament over sin have in your life, or in the life of your church? How might you do more of it, and why might that be helpful?

Lesson

EXERCISE

A PRAYER OF CONFESSION

20 MINUTES

This lesson's passage reveals part of the reason for Ezra's strength: he was quick to spend time with God in prayer. One way for you to grow as a believer is to do the same. So, this exercise will guide you through about ten minutes of silent prayer—just you with God. Ezra's prayer focused on confession, and so will yours. Like Ezra, you will not only confess sin but will also confess truths about God's holiness and his fatherly love for you (which are parts of confession that make fully confessing sin both possible and powerful).

There are five confession categories below, plus one about asking. On your own, pray silently through each of them, taking a minute or two for each category. There's space to make notes if you wish. If you finish before time is up, start going through the items again. Or if you don't finish, that's okay too—you still spent time with God. After about ten minutes, discuss your prayer experience with the group using the questions at the end of the exercise. (You won't be asked to list what sins you confessed, since not all confession of sin is appropriate to share in every group.)

Confess God's holiness. Begin by acknowledging the sacred beauty of the God you are privileged to approach in prayer, through Jesus.

- Praise God for his absolute purity and goodness.
- Praise him for his perfect love and justice.
- Praise him for his unfaltering commitment to destroy sin and evil.

Notes:

Confess your sin. Be honest with God about your wrongdoing.

- Confess your guilt for things you have done and have left undone.
- Confess your shame over those sins—how they reveal ugliness inside of you, have brought shame on Jesus's name, and have harmed you and others.
- Confess how desperately you need Jesus to deal with your sin.

Notes:

Confess your sorrows. Lament not just the effects of your own sin, but also how sin and brokenness around you have harmed or troubled you. Be honest with God about your hurts.

- Share with your Father sins you have seen or hurts you have felt in the world, or in your community.
- Share sins you have seen or hurts you have felt in your family.
- Share sins you have seen or hurts you have felt in the church, or while on mission for God.

Notes:

Confess God's goodness in salvation. Praise your God for all his wondrous works.

- Give thanks for the Father's grand plan of salvation, from creation to the coming day when your body will rise from the grave to live forever with God in a recreated world.
- Give thanks for Jesus, who fully took the punishment for all your sin and now prays for you constantly.
- Give thanks for the Holy Spirit, who works in you to train you in faith and godliness, and who is bringing the nations to Jesus.

Notes:

Confess God's goodness in your life. Praise your God for his generosity toward you.

- Thank God for a kindness he has shown you in your personal life or in your family.
- Thank God for a blessing he has brought to you or others through the church or a missionary effort.
- Thank God for a way he has been good to you in the past hour.

Notes:

Ask for God's help. Asking your Father for good gifts is a fundamental part of prayer, so even though Ezra didn't record any requests in his prayer, go ahead and tell your desires to God.

- Ask for forgiveness, a closer relationship with God, or greater assurance of his love to you in Jesus.
- Ask God to heal your hurts, meet your needs, or otherwise show you kindness.
- Ask God to help you overcome sin, work for his kingdom, and have confidence in Jesus's final victory.

Notes:

When the group is ready, talk about your time of prayer. What did you enjoy about it or find helpful?

What categories or specific items of confession were especially meaningful to you, and why?

In your prayer, you were able to name Jesus and mention specific truths about him that Ezra did not yet know. How does this make your confession even richer than Ezra's?

WRAP-UP AND PRAYER *10 MINUTES*

In your closing prayer time together, consider giving voice to some of your private prayers from the exercise that you may have wished you could share with others.

The next lesson will be on the first chapter of Nehemiah. If you are reading through all of Ezra-Nehemiah, you may want to read the end of Ezra 10 on your own before the next time you meet. That section of Scripture is a list of names of some Israelites who had married foreign women. Think of it not just as a list of guilty people, but as a list of people who repented and, in so doing, brought glory to God.

6

MISSION

BIG IDEA

God carries out his mission in the world through people who repent, pray, believe the gospel, and lay down their lives to go tell others.

BIBLE CONVERSATION *20 MINUTES*

The story begun in the book of Ezra continues in Nehemiah with the author turning his attention to phase 3 of the restoration of Jerusalem: rebuilding the city's walls. Walls were necessary both for security and to let a governor effectively keep order, but Jerusalem's walls had been in ruins since the Babylonians destroyed them more than a century earlier. The book of Nehemiah probably begins about thirteen years after Ezra led the second return to Jerusalem, still during the reign of Artaxerxes. Remember that Artaxerxes is the king who had received a letter warning him that the people of Jerusalem were rebuilding its walls (though that may not have been true), and responded by ordering that "this city be not rebuilt, until a decree is made by me" (Ezra 4:21).

At the book's start, Nehemiah himself is in Susa, one of the Persian capital cities, where he serves as cupbearer to the king. This would have made him a trusted advisor—one whose tasks included tasting the king's wine to ensure it had not been poisoned—and one familiar with the cheerful manners of court, where Persian custom excluded anything and anyone sad from the king's presence. With this in mind, have someone read **Nehemiah 1:1—2:10** aloud, or have a few readers take turns. Then discuss the questions below:

1. What grieves Nehemiah, and how similar are his concerns to things that grieve you about the church and the world today?

2. What makes Nehemiah's prayer in chapter 1 a good prayer before undertaking a mission for God, and what about it might you copy in your prayers?

3. What risks does Nehemiah take to launch his mission, and what have you seen in him that explains why he would take those risks?

****

Next, take turns reading the article aloud, switching readers at each paragraph break. Then discuss the questions that follow the article.

ARTICLE

NEHEMIAH'S REQUEST

5 MINUTES

Nehemiah began in a position of significant leadership at the Persian court, as cupbearer to the king. There he enjoyed a comfortable and relatively safe life. Yet when the news reached him about the desperate and sad situation of his compatriots who had returned to Jerusalem, the impact on Nehemiah was a sense of shame that almost a century after the first return, the major task of rebuilding the city's walls was still completely untouched. It was a key marker of a wider issue, which was that those who had returned were still experiencing significant difficulties. Nehemiah's heart was stirred by God to want to help his brothers in Jerusalem, even though that meant significant personal sacrifice.

Even as a trusted advisor, Nehemiah was taking a significant risk when he displayed negative emotions in front of the king. Nehemiah described the situation in terms the king could understand, explaining that the place of his ancestors' graves was in ruins. Care for the ancestral gravesite was a widely understood duty in the ancient world; it would be shaming to allow such a situation to continue. It may be significant (and wise) that Nehemiah avoided mentioning Jerusalem specifically by name, given the campaigning against the city that had happened recently in the Persian court.

The king followed up with the question Nehemiah must have been hoping for: "What are you requesting?" Nehemiah had clearly thought about this question ahead of time, since he not only asked the king to send him back home to rebuild his ancestral city but also asked for the specific resources he would need: safe passage for his journey and timber from the royal forests to rebuild the city walls and gates. He accompanied his petition with a heartfelt, silent prayer.

It was politically bold to ask permission to rebuild the walls and gates of a city that could potentially then rebel against the empire, especially since Artaxerxes had recently issued a decree halting building work in Jerusalem—and the kings of the Medes and Persians were famous for not changing their decrees![1] It is therefore astonishing that the king said yes to Nehemiah's request. Nehemiah understood why the king was so amenable: "The good hand of my God was upon me." This phrase has now been repeated several times in Ezra-Nehemiah, reflecting the way the Lord has consistently answered his people's humble, repentant prayers.[2]

It is a remarkable demonstration of God's sovereign power that he prevailed on successive Persian administrations to allow several key leaders to go and devote themselves to the welfare of a backwater community that must have been relatively low on the scale of the empire's priorities, supplying them with costly resources to aid their building projects. A central theme of this book is that, indeed, "The king's heart is a stream of water in the hand of the Lord; he turns it wherever he will" (Proverbs 21:1).

---

1. See Esther 1:19; Daniel 6:8
2. Ezra 7:9; 8:18

Nehemiah readily accepted the military guard provided for him by the king, even though Ezra had shunned asking for such an escort. It may be that in Nehemiah's case, since the king made the offer, it might have been considered offensive to refuse. The fact that these two men of faith made different choices shows that trust in the Lord does not preclude making use of whatever means of self-defense are available. The Lord can save by chariots and horses as easily as without them.

Nehemiah was clearly a godly and efficient planner and organizer. He identified the tasks that needed to be completed, the resources necessary to accomplish them, and the people who had the power to give him permission to carry through. His gifting was a blessing to God's people. But for Jerusalem to prosper was for God's people to prosper, while its dishonor and neglect meant dishonor for God's people as well. So Nehemiah's concern for rebuilding the walls of Jerusalem was not merely a strategic assessment of political and military needs. It was an expression of concern for the honor of his God.

Nevertheless, Nehemiah was not Jesus and his wise actions are not the gospel. Through God's grace, Nehemiah was enabled to rebuild the walls of Jerusalem and provide godly leadership in Judah for a whole generation. Subsequent generations in Jerusalem would be blessed by his faithful work of rebuilding the walls, which was a vital part of God's larger plan for Israel that would culminate in the coming of Christ. Yet the people of Jerusalem were not redeemed by Nehemiah's actions, good and appropriate though they were. Nehemiah could not give his people the new, circumcised hearts they needed most of all. Indeed, the returned community continued to struggle with many of the same sins their pre-exilic forefathers committed.

Our salvation would take the coming of another godly leader who also would fast and pray for his people, asking his heavenly Father for the resources to carry out his far more dangerous mission. Through his death and resurrection, Jesus provides the perfect righteousness that none of us have—not even Nehemiah. Like Nehemiah, we must cry out, "Even I and my father's house have sinned" (1:6). But in Jesus we have a glorious inheritance in the Jerusalem that is above, whose walls are truly unbreachable.

John Newton put it well in the last stanza of his famous hymn about the true Jerusalem, "Glorious Things of Thee Are Spoken."

> Savior, if of Zion's city,
> I through grace a member am,
>
> let the world deride or pity:
> I will glory in thy name.
>
> Fading is the worldling's pleasure,
> all his boasted pomp and show;
>
> solid joys and lasting treasure
> none but Zion's children know.

DISCUSSION *10 MINUTES*

When in your life have you prayed for God to clear the way for you to serve him in some specific role, and what has been the result? Do you pray like that often? Why or why not?

How does your excitement for the heavenly city with God compare to Nehemiah's passion for the earthly Jerusalem? What difference does excitement about heaven make in your life, and how might you build more of that excitement?

Lesson

EXERCISE

MOVING INTO MISSION

20 MINUTES

Your own role in God's mission to bring people to Jesus and advance his kingdom may involve crossing the world, like Nehemiah, or it may only mean crossing the street. But whatever God calls you to do for him, Nehemiah's method of moving into mission can be a helpful guide.

In this exercise, work on your own to examine five things Nehemiah did and how you might do the same. The first item asks you to imagine a way you might serve Jesus. It will help you complete the rest of the exercise if you think of something specific, big or small, as an example of what you might do. You aren't committing to actually do it, just to think about it for this exercise. Once you've worked through all five items, you'll have a chance to share some of your responses with the group.

Nehemiah CARES. He grieves and has concern for God's name and God's work in the world.

How do you care? What concern has God given you for telling about Jesus or for building his kingdom? (Think of just one specific idea.)

☐ I might tell _____ about Jesus.

☐ I might serve the church by _____.

☐ I might love my family or help them grow spiritually by _____.

☐ I might demonstrate the love of Jesus and his kingdom of justice and mercy by _____.

☐ Other: _____.

Nehemiah REMEMBERS THE GOSPEL. He recalls God's steadfast love, covenant promises, and commitment to dwell among his people.

How might you remember the gospel? What part of God's love for you, that is yours in Jesus, especially encourages you to love him and others?

☐ I live without guilt and shame. My sin is forgiven and God counts me righteous.

☐ It's not all up to me. The Holy Spirit is renewing me to be more like Jesus and strengthening me to serve his kingdom.

☐ I am never alone or homeless. As I serve, my Father listens to me, protects me, meets my needs, guides me, corrects me, and promises me a heavenly inheritance.

☐ Jesus will win. Serving his kingdom is hard, but his rule in the world is certain and will one day be complete.

☐ Other gospel encouragement: _____.

Explain *why* remembering this gospel truth will encourage you to serve God. _____

_____

_____

Nehemiah EXAMINES HIS HEART. He identifies ways he has been neglectful and needs to repent.

How might you examine your heart? To serve God, how might you need to repent of neglect or selfishness, or turn from trust in yourself to faith in God? _____

_____

_____

Nehemiah PRAYS. He presents the obstacles he faces—both those in his heart and those external—to his all-powerful God.

How might you pray? What obstacles to serving Jesus and helping to build his kingdom do you need to take before God? _____

_____

_____

Nehemiah GOES. He gets up and does something, taking risks to speak to the king, leave his comfortable life, and travel to Jerusalem.

How might you go? What big or small risks might you take, or what comforts might you give up, for the greater joy of serving Jesus? _____

_____

_____

When the group is ready, share some of your responses. How might you learn from Nehemiah as you serve God in this even greater era—as the gospel goes out to the nations?

Why might it be important not just to jump into the last item (going), but also to imitate Nehemiah in the earlier items? And why might it also be important not to do the earlier items and then put off actually going?

WRAP-UP AND PRAYER *10 MINUTES*

Include some elements from Nehemiah's prayers in your prayer time together. Praise God for his love, confess your sins, and ask him to remove obstacles that threaten to keep you from serving him.

The next lesson will take you forward to chapter 4 of Nehemiah. If you are reading though the whole book, you might want to read the rest of chapter 2 plus chapter 3 on your own before the next time you meet.

Lesson

7

BATTLING DISCOURAGEMENT

BIG IDEA

The key to battling discouragements in the Christian life is to keep our eyes fixed not only on the world's threats but especially on Jesus, who also battled discouragements but still brings victory.

BIBLE CONVERSATION *20 MINUTES*

Remember that Ezra-Nehemiah is arranged in three parallel panels. Each starts with a return from exile, then depicts opposition to reconstruction efforts, and ends with God overcoming that opposition. The message is that there will be opposition whenever we undertake any significant task for God, but with his help we may still prevail.

In Nehemiah 4, the opposition is spearheaded by Sanballat, the governor of neighboring Samaria, and his sidekick, Tobiah. The Samaritans were the people who had been resettled in the land and claimed to worship the true God even though they retained elements of false worship and did not follow the biblical law of

Moses. In chapters 2 and 3, the returned exiles had begun work on Jerusalem's wall, each tackling the portion in front of his own house, and Nehemiah had asserted that these exiles were the true Israel—meaning the Samaritans were not. The exclusivity of the gospel's claims is always offensive to the world.

Have someone read **Nehemiah 4** aloud, or have a few readers take turns. Then discuss the questions below:

1. The believers working on the wall first suffer ridicule and then face active threats. Which of these taunts or dangers feel familiar to you, and why?

2. In verse 9, Nehemiah both prays and posts guards. Where else do you see him practice both faith in God and prudent action, and how might his example apply to conflicts you face?

3. In this chapter, one concern is addressed only to have another pop up, and then another. What might be God's purpose in allowing this?

****

Now take turns, by paragraph, reading the article aloud. When you finish, discuss the questions that follow.

Lesson

ARTICLE

RENEWED OPPOSITION

5 MINUTES

Nehemiah's opponents first sought to discourage his efforts through mockery. Their taunts underlined the shame that was experienced by the post-exilic community over the state of their city. Has anything really changed for the people with Nehemiah's arrival?

Nehemiah's response was an imprecatory (curse-pronouncing) prayer against them. We are used to Jesus's admonition to pray *for* our enemies and those who persecute us rather than pray against them, so this prayer sounds strange in our ears. Indeed, the Old Testament also encourages God's people to love their personal enemies,[1] but Nehemiah is praying here in his official capacity as representative of the people before God. Just as a prosecutor may call for the full weight of the law to be brought down on an offender against whom he has no personal quarrel, so too a covenant mediator may cry out to God to defend his people against the assaults of their enemies. Nehemiah asked the Lord to intervene and act for the protection of his people.

It is true that in this era of grace, many more persecutors of the church are being brought to repentance and faith than was the

1. See Proverbs 25:21–22, for example

case under the old covenant. This should encourage us to pray for the salvation of our tormentors. It's why Jesus rebuked James and John when they wanted to call down fire from heaven on a Samaritan village that wouldn't receive him.[2]

Nonetheless, the reality is that all who oppose Christ in the end are heaping judgment upon themselves. It is not wrong for us to cry out to God to restrain the power of the wicked and, if they remain unrepentant, to judge them. In that sense, every time we pray the Lord's Prayer we are praying an imprecatory prayer, for when Jesus's kingdom comes it will result in the judgment of all who remain opposed to him. In this case, God answered Nehemiah's prayer not by removing the enemies (chapter 13 shows that Tobiah was a thorn in Nehemiah's side throughout his time in Jerusalem), but by stirring the hearts of the people to work eagerly on the wall. Sometimes the best answer to mockery is just to ignore it and carry on with God's work.

When the wall reached the halfway point, Sanballat and Tobiah plotted a more active intervention strategy: an alliance to fight against Jerusalem. Between Sanballat to the north, the Ammonites to the east, the Arabs to the south, and the Ashdodites to the west, Jerusalem was surrounded. Nehemiah might have the Persian king's support on paper, but Susa was far away. The attackers could claim they were merely putting down a planned revolt on the part of Nehemiah.

Even after prayer and the posting of guards, discouragement hung in the air. It came from three distinct sources: the difficulty of the work, enemies on every side, and even from friends, since those who lived in the areas closest to the Samaritan threat asked for people to be taken away from the wall-building project to protect them. In the face of this triple threat, Nehemiah

---

2. Luke 9:51–56

combined practical resourcefulness with trust in the Lord. He stationed armed defenders at vulnerable places, but also challenged the people to lift their eyes away from their own weakness—away from the difficulties and dangers: "Do not be afraid of them. Remember the Lord, who is great and awesome" (4:14).

Nehemiah's ultimate confidence did not rest in the motivational power of his speech, or his wisely-positioned guards, or the commitment of the people to fight for their homes and families—important though those elements were. His trust lay in the fact that "Our God will fight for us" (v. 20). If the Lord fought for Israel, then they need have no fear no matter how overwhelming the opposition or how challenging the assignment.

Nehemiah models for us how to battle discouragement and opposition by keeping our eyes fixed on the Lord, our great and awesome God. The God who brought his people out of Egypt and into the promised land, and then back to Jerusalem after the exile, is perfectly capable of protecting us in whatever situation we find ourselves. We may need to work hard and arm ourselves against our enemies (metaphorically, if not actually), but if God fights for us who can overcome us? Even the spiritual forces of darkness have no power over us if we take our stand equipped with the armor of God.

Yet the pattern of Jesus's own life warns us against interpreting this passage too triumphally. God is certainly capable of defending his people against all assaults, yet at the cross he handed Jesus over into the power of his enemies for them to mock and abuse and finally kill him. That death happened for us: the faithful Son endured the fate we deserve for our repeated unfaithfulness. But it also set a pattern of suffering for the Christian life. We are being conformed to the crucified Christ, "becoming like him in his death" (Philippians 3:10).

Sometimes faithful missionaries are martyred or die in accidents, diligent pastors see little fruit from their labors, and obedient Christians struggle in every aspect of life. God doesn't promise to empower all of us to succeed as Nehemiah did with his wall-building project. When it is his will, he is still able to do so, of course. However, he often empowers us instead to endure weakness and "failure" along the road to humbling us and making us more like Christ, which is always his ultimate goal.

None of that suffering will ever be wasted, for through it we will come to know more deeply our own powerlessness and the all-surpassing grace of God, which is sufficient even for broken sinners like us. And the gates of hell will not prevail against God's kingdom, which will certainly come in due season, bringing with it the glory that is ours in Christ.

DISCUSSION *10 MINUTES*

What types of prayer in Nehemiah's life are also part of your life, and what types of prayer do you ignore? Explain why, if you can.

Do you tend to wallow in the discouragements of living for God, or are you more likely to act as if everything is always rosy? How might you benefit from better recognizing both sides?

7

EXERCISE

REMEMBER THE LORD

20 MINUTES

The article mentioned Philippians 3:10–11. That passage explains the result of giving up your own efforts to prove yourself right with God, and instead being counted righteous through faith in Jesus: "That I may know [Christ] and the power of his resurrection, and may share his sufferings, becoming like him in his death, that by any means possible I may attain the resurrection from the dead." This tells you that your Christian life, like Jesus's life, will include suffering. As you die to self-interest, engaging the hard work of serving God and loving others, there will be hardships and opposition. But this lowly connection to Jesus is also your new-life glory, and an end to suffering awaits you at your coming resurrection.

This exercise will help you do as Nehemiah urged and "remember the Lord," especially your connection to Jesus both in suffering and in resurrection. Each item below mentions one of the difficulties Nehemiah faced. You'll consider how much you feel that same burden as you serve God and love others in big and small ways. You'll also read how Jesus faced that burden in his life—your suffering is part of your unbreakable connection to *him*! Work on your own first. Then discuss the questions at the end of the exercise.

The burden of MOCKERY. Nehemiah and his people were ridiculed for their devotion to the Lord and his work, and were despised by the people who lived around them. Living as a Christian, how much do you feel the burden of mockery and disdain?

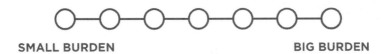

SMALL BURDEN   **BIG BURDEN**

Jesus felt the burden of mockery too: "The Pharisees, who were lovers of money, heard all these things, and they ridiculed him" (Luke 16:14).

The burden of ACTIVE PERSECUTION. Nehemiah faced very real threats to life and livelihood, and to the success of his work for God. How much do you feel the burden that your livelihood is threatened or your work hampered by persecution?

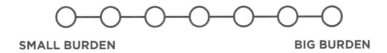

SMALL BURDEN   **BIG BURDEN**

Jesus felt the burden of persecution too: "From that day on they made plans to put him to death. Jesus therefore no longer walked openly among the Jews, but went from there to the region near the wilderness" (John 11:53–54).

The burden of DIFFICULT WORK. For the people of Jerusalem, building a wall was hard work even without persecution. In this fallen world, weariness, mistakes, unforeseen snags, limited resources, sickness and death, your own sin, and other difficulties frustrate your work. As you live for Jesus, how much do you feel the burden of these difficulties?

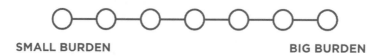

SMALL BURDEN   BIG BURDEN

Jesus felt the burden of difficult work too: "When he saw the crowds, he had compassion for them, because they were harassed and helpless, like sheep without a shepherd. Then he said to his disciples, 'The harvest is plentiful, but the laborers are few'" (Matthew 9:36–37).

The burden of DANGER TO OTHERS. Nehemiah had to deal with the fact that his work on the wall resulted in a dangerous situation for his own people who lived near Samaritan territory. Your Christian commitment may lead to dangers, hardships, disappointments, or disadvantages for people close to you. How much do you feel this burden?

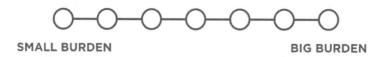

SMALL BURDEN   BIG BURDEN

Jesus felt the burden of danger to those he loved too: "The chief priests made plans to put Lazarus to death as well, because on account of him many of the Jews were going away and believing in Jesus" (John 12:10–11).

The burden of DISUNITY. Nehemiah had some of his own people come to him and call his attention away from his main task. Fellow believers who have different priorities or needs (or who don't share your zeal for the Lord's work or for obeying him) may stand in your way or abandon you. How much do you feel this burden?

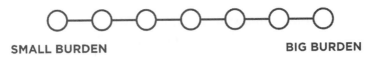

SMALL BURDEN   BIG BURDEN

Jesus felt the burden of disunity and abandonment too: "Peter took him aside and began to rebuke him. But turning and seeing his disciples, he rebuked Peter and said, 'Get behind me, Satan! For you are not setting your mind on the things of God, but on the things of man'" (Mark 8:32–33).

The second part of looking at Jesus is noticing how his life's trajectory took him *through* suffering to end in triumph:

> He was manifested in the flesh,
> vindicated by the Spirit,
> seen by angels,
>
> proclaimed among the nations,
> believed on in the world,
> taken up in glory. (1 Timothy 3:16)

Joined to Jesus, your life too will lead through suffering and death, to glory. Select some of Jesus's victories—which will also be true of you—that especially encourage you.

☐ **"Manifested in the flesh."** Even when I suffer and appear to fail in this world, I am witnessing to the humility of Jesus and demonstrating the any-cost worth of following him.

❑ **"Vindicated by the Spirit."** Although my own sin has often messed up my work for God, his power will raise me from the dead and I will be declared perfectly righteous in Jesus.

❑ **"Seen by angels."** By serving God and loving others, I am participating in Jesus's work, which will be celebrated eternally in heaven.

❑ **"Proclaimed among the nations."** This current era of wide-spread gospel preaching is already a partial victory for Jesus, and to join or support it is a foretaste of his final triumph.

❑ **"Believed on in the world."** Anyone who tries to keep me or others from believing in Jesus will lose in the end, as all who belong to Jesus eventually come to him.

❑ **"Taken up in glory."** My death will not be my end, but rather the beginning of a more glorious life with Jesus forever.

When your group is ready, share and explain some of your responses. How does the pattern of Jesus's life encourage you when you are discouraged? What difference does it make that final victory is assured?

WRAP-UP AND PRAYER *10 MINUTES*

Follow Nehemiah's example and pray for God's protection as you serve him and for his work to go forward.

The next lesson will cover Nehemiah 8. If you are reading through all of Ezra-Nehemiah, you may want to read chapters 5–7 on your own before the next time you meet.

8

THE JOY OF
THE LORD

BIG IDEA

God's Word should cause us to be in awe of his holiness and
to weep over our sin, and then to find joy in Jesus who saves
us from that sin.

BIBLE CONVERSATION *20 MINUTES*

In chapters 8–10 of Nehemiah, God's people gather to renew
the covenant. As governor, Nehemiah's concerns included spiritual reform. Like godly kings before the exile, he took initiative
in assembling the people so spiritual renewal could take place.[1]
Nehemiah's assembly is the highlight of his religious leadership
of the community of returned exiles. Before you start reading
about it, let's catch up on what has happened since Nehemiah
dealt with opposition to wall construction in chapter 4.

- In chapter 5, Nehemiah shows concern for the poor
  and ensures that those God freed from exile would live
  freely in the land. He stops the practice of debt slavery,

---

1. Previous godly reforms led by a king are described in 2 Chronicles 15:8–15; 19:4–11; 24;
29—31; 33:15–17; 34:1—35:19.

foregoing possible personal gain. He also resists laying a heavy tax burden on the people and instead supports others out of his own private resources.

- In chapter 6, Nehemiah survives an attempt on his life. In the process, he shows care not to overstep the boundaries of his office, refusing to hide in a temple area reserved for priests.

- By chapter 7, the construction of the wall is completed and Jerusalem is secured, and the people all settle in their towns.

The assembly under Nehemiah takes place alongside the Feast of Booths (or Shelters), which was also celebrated back in Ezra 3 (see lesson 2). Have someone read **Nehemiah 8** aloud, or have a few readers take turns, and then discuss the questions below:

1. Based on the details given, how would you describe the tone of the gathering, and what do you appreciate about it?

2. What actions do Ezra, Nehemiah, and the other leaders take during the assembly that are still good practices for our worship services today, or reflect good principles for us to follow? Explain.

3. How do the people show their hunger for God's Word, and how does it compare to the devotion to God's Word you see in churches today?

****

Next, take turns by paragraph reading the article aloud. Then discuss the questions that follow.

Lesson

ARTICLE

A HOLY DAY OF JOY

5 MINUTES

The Feast of Shelters was one of three great feasts on the annual Israelite religious calendar. Since it was a reenactment of the wilderness wanderings, it was ironic to celebrate it immediately after the Israelites had settled in their towns. It was yet another reminder that the land to which they had so recently returned was not their promised eternal home.

The people gathered in unity and asked Ezra to read to them from the law of Moses. Many of the people could not read, and even if they could, they would not have been able to afford their own Torah scroll. For four hours(!), Ezra read the Hebrew text aloud while some of the Levites either translated it into Aramaic, which for most of the exiles would now have been their first language, or perhaps divided it into paragraphs they explained to the people. Either way, the key point is that the reading of Scripture was done in a way that enabled the people to grasp what was being said.

The people's response to the reading of God's law was to weep, presumably as they recognized they came far short of keeping it. To discover suddenly that there were vast areas in which the community was failing to obey God's Word would have been overwhelming. Such failures had earlier led to the exile of God's people to Babylon. Yet Ezra and Nehemiah reassured the people that as a festival day holy to the Lord, this was not a day for weeping and mourning but rather one for joy and gladness. It was a day to eat and drink, celebrating God's goodness despite their sin. The joy of the Lord would strengthen them to face on another day the challenges that had been read and preached to them.

The note of celebration carried forward into the feast, which was regularly marked out by joy. Here was an opportunity right away to put into effect one of the laws they had heard Ezra read by making temporary shelters out of tree branches and camping in them, reminding themselves of the days in the wilderness. Coming amid their many difficulties establishing a renewed community in the promised land, it was a powerful testimony that God's people had been there before—about to enter the land after rebellion and judgment in the wilderness. During the seven days of the feast, Ezra continued to read from the book of the law, day after day. Surely this warned the people of God's holiness and the law's demands, but also reminded them of God's compassionate grace and the provision he had made for their sin to be forgiven, shown in the sacrificial system.

Whenever God's people take his Word seriously, it is a life-changing moment. The Reformation began when men like Martin Luther started to read and reread the Scriptures and allow them to challenge long-held notions about how we are made right with God. The Reformation spread when they started telling others about what they had found and began translating God's Word into the language of the people, so people could read it for themselves.

The initial response to discovering what God requires of his people is usually sorrowful repentance, which is appropriate.

We are sinners who have all fallen far short of God's perfect will. Yet somber reflection on our sin must soon give way to joy because of the good news of the gospel. God's Word wounds us in order to heal us, by pointing us to the gospel. Yes, we are great sinners, but Jesus Christ is a great Savior for great sinners!

This passage challenges us to examine the tone in our own worship services. There should be times when we read the Word of God and we are sobered and saddened by the conviction of sin. Sadly, there are many in our churches who are as unfamiliar with the Bible as Ezra's audience was, but they are not typically clamoring for a four-hour reading of the works of Moses, followed by an interpretation seminar. If they did, we might see more conviction of sin in our day.

Yet the fundamental note of our worship services should be joy and not sadness. I have attended services where I found myself asking "Who died?" The answer is perhaps obvious—Jesus died—but the people there seemed to have forgotten that he also rose from the dead and ascended into heaven! He has conquered sin and death and hell, and he will return again to judge the living and the dead. This news speaks to us in our appropriate sorrow over our sin and lifts our hearts to gladness and joy.

God gave his people the Jewish festival calendar to encourage them to look back to the events of the exodus and the wilderness wanderings, and to encourage them to look onward to the day when they would no longer be aliens and strangers here but would receive their full inheritance in the heavenly promised land. Some Christians find that annual celebrations like Christmas and Easter help to refocus their attention on the great events of redemptive history. Others try to remember these realities Sunday by Sunday.

For all of us, there should be times of feasting and celebration when we remember God's great acts of deliverance for us through Jesus Christ, as we do whenever we celebrate the Lord's Supper. Since we are outsiders who have been brought into God's family by grace, it is fitting for some of our feasts that we should also include the poor and the lonely, drawing them into the spiritual family of God's children with us. The church is called to be family for those who have no family of their own. What is more, our celebrations should be crowned by a longing for the fullness of our spiritual inheritance, so that we say to each other as we celebrate, "Next year in the new Jerusalem! Come soon, Lord Jesus, and claim your kingdom!"

DISCUSSION *10 MINUTES*

What is done in your family, or in your church, to remember the "wilderness" God has brought you through and the promised land he is giving you? What is helpful about these practices?

When you read the Bible or hear biblical preaching, are you more likely to neglect weeping or to neglect rejoicing? Explain why, if you can.

THE PATH TO JOY

20 MINUTES

For the people at Nehemiah's assembly, hearing about God's holiness and his beautiful commands led first to sorrow for sin (weeping). Then, as they were reminded of God's saving love (the feast day), their weeping led to renewed faith and joy. This is a model for spiritual growth.[2]

Learning more about God

Weeping

Deeper faith and joy

However, often your own life won't follow this pattern so easily. You may stall along the way to joy. Maybe you fail to weep over your sin. Or you might follow up your weeping by trying to perform better for God or by pretending to be better than you are—instead of with faith in Jesus. So, your actual path to joy includes several dead ends and looks more like this:

---

2. For a different visual look at the ideas in this exercise, see the cross diagram in session 10 of *Sonship* (Greensboro, NC: New Growth Press, 2013), 153, or in lesson 1 of Robert H. Thune and Will Walker's *The Gospel-Centered Life* (Greensboro, NC: New Growth Press, 2011), 18–20.

Complete this exercise by reading about the items in the chart, including the dead ends where your spiritual growth might stall. Note parts that sound true of you. Everyone has times of stalled growth, so be honest with yourself about both the good and bad. At the end of the exercise, you'll answer a few questions and share some of what you noticed.

LEARNING MORE ABOUT GOD. Through Bible study, preaching, or other exposure to God's Word, you gain a greater appreciation for God's holiness and goodness. You also see more clearly how he calls you to live and how deep your sin actually goes. This gulf between God's holy demands and your sinfulness seems to grow the more you learn.

NO WEEPING. Although you hear about God's holiness and sense your sinfulness, you keep from being impacted by it.

- You might dismiss obedience to God as too "legalistic" or not fitting the kind of God you wish to believe in.
- You might ignore the gulf between you and God as too daunting to deal with.
- You might resist sorrow over your sin because you're too proud to weep, or too proud to have your ideas about God corrected by his Word.
- You might depersonalize God's Word ("That's an interesting point the Bible makes"), or you put yourself over it ("I already knew that"), rather than feel the weight of truly submitting to it.

Result: Your spiritual growth stalls. You are closing yourself off to knowing God more deeply.

WEEPING. What you've learned leads to awe for God's holiness and sorrow over your sin. You are on the path to spiritual growth.

PERFORMING. Instead of trusting Jesus, you try to bridge the widening gap you see between God's holiness and your sin with your own efforts to perform better—like the Pharisees in Jesus's day.

- You might think of yourself as someone better than you actually are, or be quick to judge others.
- You might pick some outward ways to obey God that feel doable (ignoring deeper obedience), and focus on those as a way to feel superior or okay about yourself.
- You might come to a point where you realize your efforts aren't good enough, so that you get stuck in worry or despair.

- You might be guilt-ridden but still hoping to be good enough for God based on some conversion experience, outward deeds, or religious feelings.

Result: Your spiritual growth stalls. You aren't ready to learn more about God because that would only increase your burden, so Bible study and preaching become wearisome. Prayer becomes part of your performance rather than a comfort.

PRETENDING. Instead of trusting Jesus, you try to hide the gap between you and God by pretending to be better than you are.

- You might make excuses for your sin, discount its severity, or shift blame to others.
- You might be quick to explain that God's holiness doesn't really require what it seems to require, or that a little sin is no big deal.
- Your initial reaction to any suggestion you've done wrong might be to defend yourself, or you might lack honest relationships that are open about dealing with sin.
- You might be fearful of any work for God that will expose you or take you out of comfortable settings where you've learned to look like a capable believer.

Result: Your spiritual growth stalls. Learning more about God is little more than a way to show off, or it threatens your image, so Bible study becomes either self-serving or uncomfortable. Prayer feels fake.

BELIEVING THE GOSPEL. Along with seeing how God is more holy and you are more sinful than you ever thought, you also see how Jesus is a bigger and more compassionate Savior than you ever dared imagine.

- You learn to judge your status with God by how much Jesus has done for you, not how much you've done for him—which frees you from fear.
- You learn to take your sins to Jesus for cleansing and know that you are loved, forgiven, counted righteous, adopted by God, empowered to serve, and made an heir to Jesus's kingdom.
- Your obedience to God flows from gratitude, joy, love, confidence in his work in you, and hope in the future Jesus guarantees.
- You are able to truly love others because your eyes are on Jesus more than on yourself.

Result: You have true spiritual growth. You are ready to go back to the top of the diagram to learn more about God and wrestle more deeply with your sin, and then grow a still bigger appreciation for Jesus—and enjoy life with God!

When the group is ready, share some of what you noticed about your life. What parts of the chart represent places your spiritual life has often been? Explain.

What progress has God helped you make in avoiding some of the dead ends where your spiritual growth might stall? Tell about it.

Why is it important that preaching and Bible studies include proclaiming the gospel of Jesus? How can you make sure you see Jesus when you learn from the Bible?

WRAP-UP AND PRAYER *10 MINUTES*

God gives spiritual growth. Ask your Father to help your understanding of Jesus and your appreciation for him grow.

9

TRUE REPENTANCE

BIG IDEA

As God's people, we should be sorrowful about sin, yet joyful about Jesus.

BIBLE CONVERSATION *20 MINUTES*

In our last lesson, the people responded to God's law by weeping over their sin. But the Feast of Booths was a time for joy, not sorrow, so they stopped weeping and instead celebrated God's promises and how he had begun to fulfill them. Now in Nehemiah 9, the time to mourn their sin arrives. The feast is over, and the people gather to express repentance. In the Bible, repentance is an inner action: a recognition of sin and heartfelt sorrow over it, and a resolve to turn from sin and toward God. Ongoing repentance is a grace from God and part of a believer's lifestyle.

The Levites will lead the people in a lengthy prayer of repentance, recorded for us as a model for our own prayers of repentance. As it turns out, the people will be confessing much history—both the history of their sin and the history of God's faithfulness.

Have someone read **Nehemiah 9** aloud, or have several readers take turns. Then discuss the questions below:

1. What do you find good about the people's approach leading up to the prayer of confession, and why?

2. What do you appreciate about the things they say—what they confess about themselves, and what they profess is true of God? Why is saying these things an important part of repentance.

3. How do you react to the people writing and signing a promise to obey God's law (explained in more detail in chapter 10)? Does this action feel godly, or is it rash and overconfident?

****

Now read the article aloud, taking turns by paragraph. Then discuss the questions at the end of the article.

A REPENTANT PEOPLE

5 MINUTES

It is striking that the prayer of repentance in Nehemiah 9 takes a while to get to any mention of the peoples' own sin. Instead, it begins with a call to praise God, which sets the immediate moment and its concerns in the larger scope of what God is up to in redemptive history. From beginning to end, the story of the world is the unfolding of God's glorious name—his character—so that humanity may join in praising God for who he is and what he has done: "Stand up and bless the LORD your God from everlasting to everlasting" (v. 5).

The prayer's survey of redemptive history includes most of the key moments up to that point in time:

- The Lord created all things and sustains them, and has kept his covenant promises to Abraham.
- The Lord saved his people from Egypt and provided for them in the wilderness.
- The Lord declared himself "gracious and merciful, slow to anger and abounding in steadfast love," even though the people were unfaithful and untrusting.

- The Lord brought his people into the promised land and allowed them to suffer when their patterns of rebellion continued, but always gave them saviors when they cried out to him. After he gave rest from their enemies, they would rebel again. But even after the exile, he did not forsake them.

When the Levites' prayer reaches the present moment, it describes the remnant people of Israel as being in great distress—slaves in the land the Lord promised to give to their fathers to enjoy. This is not due to any failure on God's part. He has dealt faithfully with them. Yet, because of the people's sin, the Lord's faithfulness meant the judgment of exile. In a sense, this exile was ongoing for those who had returned to rebuild their land. The rich yield of their fields went to their Persian overlords, and they were left with little or nothing.

Based on history, it was time for the Lord to send another deliverer to redeem his people. But before that could happen, it was time for the people to humble themselves, repent, and commit to lives of obedience to the Lord, trusting that he would provide for their needs as he had done so many times before. The returnees did this by renewing their covenant with the Lord, committing themselves once again to serve God. They acknowledged that he alone was their true king and master. In chapter 10, they will demonstrate this commitment by vowing to bring to the temple the tithes, firstfruits, first dough, and all the other commitments laid upon them by the Sinai covenant. Nehemiah himself will be first to sign the document.

What should we make of this prayer and the covenant that everyone subsequently subscribed to? Does it mean that whenever we wish to repent of our sins, we should likewise sign a sworn statement never to do it again? No, if their intent had been to place their hope in their own sworn resolve, it would have been naïve to say the least, given the long history of failure on the part of previous generations of Israelites, highlighted prominently in the prayer itself!

The desire expressed in the renewed covenant to be done with all known sin certainly was a good one, and it is godly for us as well to declare our desire to repent of sin—especially the particular sins that beset us so closely. But the reality is that before the book of Ezra-Nehemiah finishes, the new covenant they made will have been broken every bit as surely as the Sinai covenant had been. Their hope could never rest in their commitment to do the right thing.

Instead, their hope rested where it always had: in the character and faithfulness of God, the glorious name that has been his identifying feature from everlasting and will remain the same through everlasting ages. This is why we are to stand up and bless the Lord even though we are still covered with the dirt and sackcloth of our acknowledged sin and brokenness. It is because he is a gracious and merciful God, slow to anger and abounding in steadfast love, forgiving our wickedness and iniquity and transgression. He even forgives the many sins we continue to commit as Christians, as we stubbornly prefer our own foolishness to the wisdom of obeying his law.

To achieve our deliverance, the Lord would raise up another Savior: the God-man, Jesus Christ, who alone gives us lasting rest. Jesus brings a new covenant of his own, not signed and sealed in the best intentions of human beings but signed and sealed in his own blood, poured out for the remission of sins. In this new covenant, he commits himself to provide the perfect righteousness we could never achieve. He merits on our behalf the spiritual blessings pointed to at Sinai.

United to Jesus, we receive the gift of the indwelling Spirit, who continues to convict us of our sins, call us to repentance, and give us godly joy in the forgiveness that is ours in Christ. Step by step, the Spirit draws us along the path to new obedience, as is fitting for those who are God's people. We put off our old, sinful ways and put on Christ instead.

We are all exiles in an alien land, distressed over our sin and the ungodliness that mars our hearts. We long for our true home in heaven. But as we wait, we can recite the prayer of Nehemiah 9 to remind us that this state of affairs is normal, and that our faithful God will not abandon us until he has created a new, holy people who are fit for a blessed eternity with him in Christ.

DISCUSSION *10 MINUTES*

Do you often mourn deeply over your sin? When you do, what does that look like?

How might you proclaim repentance to the nations (or to your neighbor) in a way that's winsome and humble?

GRACE TO THE HUMBLE

20 MINUTES

James 4:6 says about repentance, "God opposes the proud, but gives grace to the humble." This shows that (1) true repentance is not proud but humble, and (2) humble repentance brings grace from God into your life. In this exercise, work on your own to complete two parts, one for each of those points. Then discuss the questions at the end as a group.

PART 1: Proud vs. humble. The chart below gives some of the differences between a false repentance that remains proud and a true repentance that's humble. Read through the items and note a few that are meaningful to you (perhaps they are especially true of you, or show how you've grown, or reflect how you want to grow).

PROUD "REPENTANCE"	HUMBLE REPENTANCE
Full of excuses. "You see, I was tired . . . what he did made me angry . . . I had good intentions at the start . . . etc."	**Free of excuses.** "That was wrong of me, period."
Ignoring the past. "Yes, I sinned—this time."	**Acknowledging the past.** "I've been like this repeatedly, for a long time."

PROUD "REPENTANCE"	HUMBLE REPENTANCE
Sorry for consequences. "I've learned my lesson."	**Sorry for spurning God.** "I've failed to love my Father."
Failing to see that sin is horrible. "I'm still better than others. Besides, the way I am is not all my fault."	**Appropriately horrified by sin.** "The way I am dishonors my Savior, and that bothers me. Praise God that Jesus took my shame and removed it when he died for me on the cross!"
Shallow. "Okay, I'm sorry for how I behave sometimes."	**Deep.** "I hate my underlying selfishness and coldness."
Resentful toward God. "I hope I've changed enough and felt sorry enough to satisfy God."	**Delighting in mercy.** "I cherish the fact that my tears stir Jesus's compassion."
External. "It'll be hard, but I'm going to change a few outward behaviors."	**Internal.** "I have a new awareness of sin and a bottom-line desire to serve Jesus—even when it's hard or I'm not feeling it at the moment."
Self-effort-based. "I'll show God how much better I can be."	**Reliance-based.** "I truly want God to make me better."
Barren of faith. "All I can see is what a sinner I am. I'm hopelessly broken."	**Coupled with faith.** "God has always come to restore his repentant people. Yes, I'm broken, but in Christ I'm also beautiful."

PART 2: Grace for the humble. You can see that true repentance is hard. It can feel like death, because it is death to your old self (Colossians 3:5–10), so that you might think of it only as a burden. For this reason, it's important to see that repentance is actually a *gospel blessing* that leads to lasting joy. Before the gospel was announced, Adam and Eve were only told, "If you eat from the tree, you will surely die." But the gospel brings sweet grace: "If you repent in your heart, you will surely live."

Below, read some brief Bible passages that tell of the blessings found in repentance. Note or underline some phrases that might encourage you to repent even though repentance is hard.

Complete mercy and forgiveness. "I acknowledged my sin to you, and I did not cover my iniquity; I said, 'I will confess my transgressions to the LORD,' **and you forgave the iniquity of my sin**" (Psalm 32:5).

God's full acceptance and delight in you. "The sacrifices of God are a broken spirit; a broken and contrite heart, O God, you will not despise" (Psalm 51:17).

Powerful prayer. "The LORD **has heard the sound of my weeping.** The LORD **has heard my plea; the** LORD **accepts my prayer**" (Psalm 6:8–9).

Spiritual growth and nearness to Jesus. "Those whom I love, I reprove and discipline, so be zealous and repent. Behold, I stand at the door and knock. If anyone hears my voice and opens the door, I will come in to him and eat with him, and he with me" (Revelation 3:19–20).

Readiness for mission and Jesus's return. "Repent therefore, and turn back, that your sins may be blotted out, that times of refreshing may come from the presence of the Lord, and that he may send the Christ appointed for you, Jesus, whom heaven must receive until the time for restoring all the things about which God spoke by the mouth of his holy prophets long ago" (Acts 3:19–21).

Joy in heaven. "There will be more joy in heaven over one sinner who repents than over ninety-nine righteous persons who need no repentance" (Luke 15:7).

When the group is ready, share some of your results. What items are meaningful or helpful to you, and why?

How might your attitude about repentance need to change, and how might you live differently if it did?

WRAP-UP AND PRAYER *10 MINUTES*

Spend time praying for repentance. True repentance is hard, but you have God's power on your side—and he loves to see you repent. Ask him for that grace in your life.

The next lesson will skip ahead to Nehemiah 13. If you are reading through all of Ezra-Nehemiah, you might want to read Nehemiah 10–12 on your own before your next meeting.

Lesson

10

LASTING REFORMATION

BIG IDEA

Since reforms and renewal often do not last, they are a constant struggle for us and for the church while we are in this world—but Jesus is bringing change that endures.

BIBLE CONVERSATION *20 MINUTES*

After the ceremony of repentance in Nehemiah 9, the people signed a document promising to keep God's laws. Chapter 10 mentions several specifics: no intermarriage, no buying and selling on the Sabbath day of rest and worship, and the giving of tithes and offerings to support the priests and Levites who ministered at the temple. In chapter 11, the underpopulation of Jerusalem is addressed with a transfer of residents from other towns. And then in chapter 12, the city's newly repaired walls are dedicated, "and the joy of Jerusalem was heard far away" (12:43).

Chapter 13 will begin with the reappearance of Tobiah the Ammonite, who taunted the wall builders in chapter 4, and with the realization that the people are not following a law given in Deuteronomy 23:3–6, which excludes Ammonites and Moabites from the assembly of Israel because of how their ancestors opposed God's people during the wilderness period. It's important to remember that this was not a racial exclusion, but a religious one. Ammonites and Moabites shared a physical lineage with Israel, but they worshiped false gods known for child sacrifice. There had always been an exception for those such as Ruth the Moabite who renounced their nationality and religion. Ruth's great-grandson King David himself was of mixed descent, but there was nothing ambiguous about his commitment to the Lord, and David clearly was not excluded from the assembly.

Have someone read **Nehemiah 13** aloud, or have several readers take turns. Then discuss the questions below:

1. What are the main problems Nehemiah discovers when he returns to Jerusalem, and how are they similar to problems present among believers today?

2. List several ways that living among large groups of unbelievers makes obeying God more challenging for the people. How is your situation similar, and what does this chapter teach you about how to respond?

3. What do you think of Nehemiah's enforcement methods in verses 25–27? What do you appreciate about those methods, and what might be lacking?

****

Now read this study's final article, taking turns reading it aloud. Then discuss the questions that follow.

Lesson

ARTICLE

THEY DID NOT LIVE HAPPILY EVER AFTER

5 MINUTES

If Hollywood were to film the narrative of Ezra-Nehemiah, you may be sure that it would not include Nehemiah 13. The reason is simple: it's such a downer. At the end of chapter 12, we are ready for the Hollywood ending: "So they lived happily ever after." But they didn't. In chapter 13, we discover that as soon as Nehemiah left Jerusalem to report back to King Artaxerxes, all of his and Ezra's achievements started to fall apart. To his credit, Nehemiah set things straight on his return. But we are left wondering what will happen to these reforms after the death of Nehemiah. If leaders like Ezra and Nehemiah can't reform God's people in a way that lasts, who can?

Just recently, the people had made an apparently sincere and firm commitment to spiritual reform. Now Nehemiah had to deal with several threats to that reform:

Corruption of worship. Idol worshipers still loyal to their false-god heritage were being allowed into the assembly of the Lord's people. This issue was highlighted by Eliashib the priest providing a room in the temple itself for the use of his relative, Tobiah the Ammonite. Earlier, Tobiah had made himself a vocal enemy of the reforms in Judah. Now the holy articles that were supposed to have been stored in the temple were displaced—to make room for a pagan! Couldn't the people see that the worship of a holy God must be pure and free of evil influences? Why couldn't zeal for undefiled worship be something that lasts?

Neglect of ministers. The misuse of a room for Tobiah was symptomatic of a wider problem. The provisions for the Levites were not being maintained, with the result that they had to go back to working their fields rather than being free to fulfill their duties as temple singers and gatekeepers. They were supposed to be supported through the tithes, firstfruits, and offerings of the people, but they had been neglected. Couldn't the people see that they were robbing God and his temple? Why couldn't support for godly ministry be something that lasts?

Breaking of the Sabbath. The Sabbath was a particularly sensitive issue in the returned community, since a failure to keep the Sabbath was one of the key sins that led to the exile.[1] How could the remnant survive if they failed in such a critical mark of obedience? The multicultural society in which they found themselves made it easy to be slack about the Sabbath. Foreign merchants who had no allegiance to the God of Israel felt free to sell on the Sabbath—and the people were complicit in buying.

The Sabbath can be a controversial subject in churches today, but it need not be if we understand it as a gift rather than a duty. It is a day given for us to set aside the necessary obligations of the remainder of the week and rest, reminding ourselves that God can provide all our needs without our aid. What luxurious freedom to remember that our heavenly Father is still in control!

---

1. 2 Chronicles 36:21; Ezekiel 20:16

In addition, it is a day to give rest to others by seeking out ways to enhance their rest on that day. That means it is a day for worshiping God and serving others along with relaxation for ourselves. It is meant to be a foretaste of heaven, not a day when we spend the whole time trying not to break a set of legalistic rules. Couldn't the people see that their neglect of the Sabbath was just robbing themselves of delight in God? Why couldn't the observance of godly rest be something that lasts?

Intermarriage. It is no surprise that intermarriage re-emerged as a pressing concern. The political and economic advantages that made it popular earlier continued to operate, and even the family of Eliashib was implicated. The result was a loss of the holy seed. Children unable to speak the Judean language would not understand the Scriptures. They would grow up unable to be part of the covenant community, unable to understand the reading of the Book of Moses. Couldn't the people see the importance of raising children to know the Lord? Why couldn't godly families be something that lasts?

Chapter 13 ends with order restored to the house and city of God through Nehemiah's prompt and forceful actions. His style was quite different from Ezra's. Instead of lamenting the people's sin and pulling out his own hair, he beat some offenders and pulled out their hair. But God used both leadership styles. Nehemiah's influence clearly was good in Jerusalem, as the book's final line argues. But the reader is still left with an uncomfortable feeling. How long after Nehemiah will these positive changes continue?

Nehemiah is not Jesus. Like the best of the kings of the Old Testament, even after all of Nehemiah's achievements for God, the people were still left short of salvation. But Nehemiah and

Ezra pointed people to the one who was to come, the one who would bring salvation and rest for his people—to King Jesus.

Jesus combines Nehemiah's toughness with Ezra's tenderness, and he balances Nehemiah's directness with Ezra's sensitivity. Only Jesus possesses this perfect blend of spiritual gifts. In his zeal for pure worship, he cleansed the temple with a whip, but he also wept over prodigal Jerusalem with the tenderness of a mother hen.[2] He denounced the religious leaders and Pharisees, yet was known as the friend of tax collectors and sinners.[3] In him, the Lion of Judah and the Lamb of God meet and merge. In him, mercy and justice embrace in perfect balance and harmony.

In Jesus, the promised new creation has already begun. It's a lasting reality in us through the Holy Spirit's ongoing work of sanctification. The ministry of the gospel is spreading to every corner of the world, and children of God are found in every nation. Surely, this good work God has begun will continue until Jesus returns. Then he will usher in pure and heavenly worship, eternal rest and delight in God, and the great family where "they shall all know me, from the least of them to the greatest" (Hebrews 8:11). This is our lasting hope and comfort as deeply broken people who inhabit a desperately broken world.

DISCUSSION *10 MINUTES*

Which most bothers you: corruption of worship, neglect of ministers, an ignored or legalistic Sabbath, or children not raised to know the Lord? How much do you think the culture you live in influences your answer?

What can you do so that the work of your spiritual leaders won't be lost the moment they retire or leave town?

---

2. John 2:14–17; Luke 13:34
3. Matthew 11:19

Lesson

EXERCISE

A PRAYER FOR CHANGE THAT LASTS

15 MINUTES

As you've studied Ezra-Nehemiah, you may have been reminded there's much in your Christian life that doesn't nec-essarily seem to last. Ministry ventures, spiritual commitments, progress against sin—in this world, all can be interrupted or come undone. For this exercise, you'll identify one area in your life where progress seems to have stopped or a blessing you once enjoyed now feels gone. Then you'll practice faith in Jesus, the only leader whose work is truly lasting, by praying about it. Answer two questions below on your own, and then share and pray with your group.

Question 1: What progress or blessing in your spiritual life seems not to have lasted? It may be one of the following:

- A personal commitment to serve God or resist sin that you haven't been able to keep up, or feel yourself becoming cold or hardened toward.
- A mission effort or a project to serve God where you have faced discouragement, setbacks, or failure.

- A movement to reform or improve the church, or a strength of the church, that you fear is slipping away or might be lost.
- A godly part of the culture you live in that has been discarded or seems to be going away.
- A spiritual commitment or vitality in your family that someone you love seems to be losing or forsaking.
- A joy for Jesus or passion for his kingdom that isn't what it once was.
- A valued church home, Christian friend, fellowship group, pastor, or other Christian encouragement that you once had but can't seem to get back.
- Some other progress or blessing that seems not to have lasted.

Something that has not lasted in my spiritual life is _____
_____
_____
_____.

Question 2: How do you want to pray about it? Prayer is one of the best ways to look to Jesus in your situation. Even if God says yes to your prayer, it might not mean you get the fully lasting version of what you seek in this life (since that's sometimes reserved for the heavenly life). But you will be seeking in the right place, drawing near to the ever-living Savior whose blessings endure. You might just tell God how you're feeling, or you might ask him for one of these blessings:

- A restoration of what you once had that did not last.
- A greater blessing or new progress.
- A stronger hope in Jesus's return and the next life.

- A closer life with him as you struggle with what you've lost.
- Spiritual growth in your struggle.
- Something else, or all of these!

Something I want to pray is: _____
_____
_____
_____.

When the group is ready, briefly share your prayer items with each other. Then move on to the next section to pray about them together.

WRAP-UP AND PRAYER *15 MINUTES*

Take extended time in prayer, including each item from the exercise in your closing prayer time together.

LEADER'S NOTES

These notes provide some thoughts and background information that relate to the study's discussion questions, especially the Bible conversation sections. The discussion leader should read these notes before the study begins. Sometimes, the leader may want to refer the group to a point found here.

However, it is important that you not treat these notes as a way to look up the "right answer." The most helpful and memorable answers usually will be those the group discovers on its own through reading and thinking about the Bible text. You will lose the value of taking time to look thoughtfully at the text if you are too quick to turn to these notes.

LESSON 1: THE LORD'S WORK

The reestablishment of proper worship is perhaps the most visible purpose in Ezra 1, but other purposes of God are present as well: the participation of all his people (and even some who aren't his people), his detailed provision of all they need, and his commitment to a legacy of saving work and worship he planned and began in ages past.

Just as the Lord stirs up the spirit of Cyrus to allow the people of Judah to return home (v. 1), he also stirs the spirits of the exiles to carry out the project—both those who volunteered to be part of the first wave of the return and their neighbors who remained in Babylon. The first group commits their lives while the second group gives generously of their resources to support the costly venture. In the exodus from Egypt, Israel's Egyptian neighbors provided them with treasures to aid them on their way (Exodus

12:35–36). Here the neighbors of those going up to Jerusalem provide gold, silver, and other precious treasures to help their work—a note that casts this journey as a kind of second exodus.

Cyrus himself returns the temple vessels King Nebuchadnezzar of Babylon had taken from Jerusalem and put in the house of his gods (Daniel 1:2). These temple vessels may have been among the treasures Hezekiah showed the Babylonian envoys in Isaiah 39. In Daniel 5, these same sacred goblets and dishes were brought out by Belshazzar for his final feast in praise of pagan gods. Now the temple vessels are going home, a vital symbol of continuity between the new temple to be constructed in Jerusalem and the former temple Nebuchadnezzar had destroyed. The promises the Lord had made with respect to Solomon's temple in 1 Kings 8 would be carried forward to the new temple.

The era we live in today has seen even greater fulfillment of God's ancient promises. We have seen God's glory in Christ. We know how stunningly he has already kept many of his promises in the birth, death, resurrection, and intercessory prayers of Jesus. We enjoy the fullness of the Spirit's outpouring, the delight of the gospel preached to the whole world, and the anticipation that Christ is returning soon. All of the comforts, encouragements, and motivations God gives his people have been heightened for us.

Note that those who returned to Judea in the first wave were largely from two tribes—Judah and Benjamin—along with a number of priests and Levites (the tribe responsible for maintaining the temple and worship). Most of the exiles in Babylon came from the former Southern Kingdom, which was primarily made up of these tribes. The ten northern tribes were exiled earlier by the Assyrians who dispersed them in many different places, precluding the possibility of a similar organized return.

LESSON 2: WORSHIP

The peoples' first act of worship, attending the feast, led to the first communal rebuilding activity, the altar of the temple. Both the altar and the temple itself were important links with the past but also were new to most of the exiles, who had never been able to worship in the way God had specified. They understood that the restoration God was now bringing would begin with restored worship. The passage mentions Jeshua (Joshua) the high priest and Zerubbabel, whose leadership in the later rebuilding of the temple is recorded in Haggai and Zechariah. Zerubbabel was from the line of King David (see 1 Chronicles 3:19), another link with the past. The royal house and the priesthood provided unified leadership for the building program, unlike in times past when the two sometimes pulled in opposite directions (for example, 2 Chronicles 26:16–21).

Those who returned had to do everything exactly as required in God's law, for they remembered that failure to do so was one of the key causes that had led to the exile. Once the altar was rebuilt, it became the focus for the regular calendar of ritual offerings prescribed in the law of Moses. Daily, monthly, and annual festivals are mentioned. This too was continuity with the people of God stretching back to the exodus and beyond. It showed that God's promises to dwell in the midst of his people and be a refuge and a strength for them (Psalm 46) applied to this new generation also.

To build the temple as far as possible after the pattern given to Solomon in 1 Kings 6 required materials that were not locally available—cedar logs from Lebanon, which came via Tyre and Sidon—and the skilled craftsmen necessary to do the work. That too was an echo from the past, for Solomon had made a similar request in 2 Chronicles 2:3–9 when he built the original temple. On that occasion, Solomon funded the work out of his own resources, but the returned exiles were dependent upon the grant provided to them by Cyrus. This is an important reminder of just how dependent the returned exiles were on the good graces of the Persian authorities, which will come into play in the next lesson.

LESSON 3: FACING OPPOSITION

The offer to collaborate on building the temple came from people who worshiped the Lord as one god among many, which was no better than not worshiping him at all. As a result, Zerubbabel and Jeshua could not accept their offer. It would have tainted the whole project from the outset with precisely those sins that had earlier sent Israel into exile. This was no light matter, and the entire leadership of the Judean community was united in refusing the offer. Those God had brought home from exile were now the true heirs of the promises of "the LORD, the God of Israel" (4:3). To be acceptable to him, their worship had to be pure, which meant it had to accord with the directions of David (3:10) and the law of Moses (3:2). Who knows what the people already in the land would have wanted to include in the rebuilt temple had they helped with the project?

The letter they send later reveals the kind of opposition the returnees faced throughout this whole period. The letter uses flattery of the king and his predecessors, and it claims God's people are rebuilding Jerusalem as a prelude to rebellion. The enemies appeal to the king's profit interests, alleging the work will inevitably result in a loss of honor and revenue. They also appeal to fear, suggesting the result will be the loss of the entire province of Beyond the River, not just the tiny territory of Judah that was a part of the province. Such tactics—assigning evil motives and imagining false dangers—can feel deeply hurtful to those they are used against. They are often part of the battle waged against believers by those who are of the devil, who "has nothing to do with the truth, because there is no truth in him" (John 8:44).

It's important to draw the right parallels here in order to make the right application in our context. The relevance of this passage is not to be found in support for the modern political state of Israel; rather, the church is the contemporary people of God charged with rebuilding outposts of the heavenly Jerusalem while we await the return of our true King, Jesus, from heaven (Philippians 3:20–21). There are all kinds of ways in which we can collaborate with people who are not believers in seeking to improve our society in general, but the church is called to be a distinctly holy people with a distinctive identity within the wider community (1 Peter 2:9; 2 Corinthians 6:14–18).

LESSON 4: DEVOTION TO GOD

Ezra was an excellent choice to lead God's people. He had the scholarly credentials to be a wise and knowledgeable teacher, and a heartfelt interest in that task. He also was blessed with political wisdom and connections. Moreover, he had the spiritual wisdom to credit God when things went well, showing himself to be a man of worship and thanksgiving. In verse 28, he seems to treasure his covenant relationship with God, referring to "the LORD my God." In coming chapters, he will show himself to be a humble man of faith and fasting and prayer (Ezra 8:21–23), a man whose heart is broken by sin (Ezra 9), a man who leads his congregation in confession (Ezra 10), and one who guides his flock into true repentance (Nehemiah 9). It all makes for excellent pastoral qualities.

Artaxerxes's letter gave Ezra carte-blanche support to undertake his mission. Anyone from the Jewish community who wished to go with him could do so, echoing the permission given by Cyrus for the original return in a previous generation (compare 7:13 with 1:3). The king and his counselors provided a considerable amount of gold and silver for the temple, and he encouraged others to do likewise. This provision of gold and silver to the Jews by the surrounding people gave this return, like the first, the flavor of a new exodus, an image reinforced by the fact that the group left Babylon just two days before the beginning of the Passover festival (8:31). More temple vessels were donated by Artaxerxes, also heightening the similarities between Ezra's journey and the first return in Ezra 1. This was another new beginning for the Jewish community, and although Artaxerxes saw it as a way to gain favor with one of the gods, Ezra knew it was really the work of the one true God.

Ezra was indeed blessed by Artaxerxes's support. Sometimes God gives us similarly wise and favorable leaders, and when he does, we should give him thanks as Ezra did. Leaders don't necessarily have to be Christians to do what is right. God can steer their hearts to do the right thing at any moment. Yet at other times God sovereignly places his people under harsh and repressive regimes, such as the same Persian Empire a few years later during the time of Haman in the book of Esther. God is in control both when he rescues his people from danger and when he allows them to be martyred as witnesses for him. Both circumstances give them the opportunity to trust and glorify him in the face of an adverse world.

LESSON 5: LAMENT OVER SIN

Try not to let this lesson turn into a discussion about marriage and divorce, which is not the main point of the passage. However, your group may wonder why Ezra supports putting away unbelieving wives while Paul says in 1 Corinthians 7:12–15 not to divorce an unbeliving spouse unless they force the issue. If this comes up, note that the two situations are different:

- The marriages described in Ezra may be too tainted to preserve. They might be mere marriages of convenience, or exploitative, or defiled by ongoing participation in idolatrous temple rites. This was less likely the case in Corinth.
- The marriages in Ezra are clearly illegal according to God's law, perhaps making them illegitimate in the first place because the men intentionally married unbelievers knowing this was forbidden. In Corinth, it's more likely that two unbelievers were already married (which is a legitimate marriage) when one of them became a believer later. That marriage remains legal in God's eyes.
- It may be significant that the situation in Ezra addresses Israelite men married to foreign women, whereas Paul has in view believing men *and* women married to unbelieving spouses. It would be easier for the believing men who sent away wives to have made adequate provision for them as they left, whereas a believer who abandoned an unbelieving husband would likely have been left without support.
- God's people may have reached a greater maturity in Paul's age, resulting in the need for a slightly different practice (see Matthew 19:3–9 for Jesus's comments on the Old Testament divorce allowances given in Deuteronomy 24:1–4). With the pouring out of the Spirit on all nations (Acts 2), there is more hope now of seeing an outsider come to faith in the living God. Notice, though, that Paul still says it is completely wrong for a believer to go ahead and marry an unbeliever. We may not presume upon God's grace: "How do you know, wife, whether you will save your husband? Or how do you know, husband, whether you will save your wife?" (1 Corinthians 7:16).
- Throughout the Old Testament period, there is an emphasis on God's people being a holy lineage leading to the Messiah. The people's blatant disregard for this lineage

is not just disobedience of God's law but also defiance against his plan of salvation, making it right for Ezra to take drastic action. In a sense, the intermarriage is a devilish ploy to extinguish Jesus's ancestors by assimilation.

In any case, the emphasis in Ezra is not on what situations allow for divorce, but on the need to obey God's word and the value of confession and repentance when we do not. Ezra shows his godliness in being a man who "trembled at the words of the God of Israel" (9:4) and leading others to gather around him and do the same. The phrasing recalls the Lord's words in Isaiah 66:2, "But this is the one to whom I will look: he who is humble and contrite in spirit and trembles at my word."

Notice that Ezra bases his confession not only on what the people have done, but also on what he knows about God and Israel's history with God. Ezra acknowledges that these same sins led to Israel's exile in accordance with the curses of the Sinai covenant (see Leviticus 26). Israel's entire history was a long catalog of transgressions, and Ezra recognizes that it was because of these past sins that Judah was still in slavery in his own day, under the yoke of the Persians (Ezra 9:9). Yet he also thanks God for the measure of freedom and rest they had been given, and for the remnant that returned to Jerusalem and rebuilt the temple. They were not completely free, but they had more freedom than they had any right to expect.

LESSON 6: MISSION

The news that the walls of Jerusalem were in disrepair can hardly have been entirely new information to Nehemiah, yet he allows himself to feel its impact. Much like Ezra did when he heard of the people's sin, so too Nehemiah weeps and fasts before the Lord when he hears about Jerusalem. He laments both the plight of his people and their part of the responsibility for it—even though it appears their current sin was mostly limited to neglect. Most importantly, he does not hold in his sorrow but takes it to God.

Nehemiah's prayer is similar to Solomon's prayer at the dedication of the original temple in 2 Chronicles 6:14–40. He appeals to God's covenant and steadfast love (compare 1:5 to 2 Chronicles 6:14). He asks that the Lord's ears and eyes might be attentive and open to his plea (compare 1:6 to 2 Chronicles 6:40). Nehemiah also confesses Israel's sins, including his own sins and those of his father's house, realizing that the people had repeatedly rebelled against the commandments the Lord gave through Moses (1 Kings 8:53, 58).

Not coincidentally, the focus of Nehemiah's prayer is the precise situation that was envisaged in Solomon's prayer in 2 Chronicles 6:36–39. The people had sinned against the Lord and were taken into exile, where they humbled themselves and repented, praying to the Lord for help. Specifically, Nehemiah asks for mercy (*rachamim*) from God before King Artaxerxes, while Solomon had asked God to show *rachamim* to the people before their conquerors in 1 Kings 8:50. The expectation is that such a humble, repentant prayer will receive the answer promised to Solomon in 2 Chronicles 7:14. God will hear from heaven, forgive his people's sin, and heal their land. The situation in our day, as we live under the fullness of the gospel, is even more brimming with hope. The humble, daily repentance of God's people is a powerful witness to Jesus wherever the gospel is preached.

It is not surprising that Nehemiah, a man of repentance and faith, would dare to speak before the king and travel to Jerusalem. Those familiar with his story may know that later in chapter 2, after arriving in Jerusalem, Nehemiah also goes out at night to inspect the city's walls secretly, likely because he realizes there will be strong opposition to his rebuilding plan. None of these risks stop him. Nehemiah knows he serves a greater King who offers greater glory, even if outward conditions will appear less regal than life in the Persian court.

EXERCISE: There is a two-way connection between growing in the gospel and going out on mission for God. On the one hand, the truths of the gospel and the repentance and faith that flow from those truths will propel us out to serve God and love others. If we aren't gospel-motivated, our "going" will probably be selfish, fake, powerless, or joyless. On the other hand, without actually going we might never see much reason to dive deeply into gospel truths and draw closer to Jesus. So, the hard work of mission also propels us back to the gospel, repentance, and faith—where we are renewed again to keep going. If we aren't goers, our gospel pursuit will probably be shallow or coldly academic. The final question in the exercise is meant to help your group discuss this dynamic.

LESSON 7: BATTLING DISCOURAGEMENT

The mockery in Nehemiah 4 is directed both at the people themselves ("these feeble Jews") and their work ("A fox could break it down!"). Sanballat and Tobiah also tried to make the people lose sight of the end of the project, claiming they would never reach the culmination when sacrifices of thanksgiving would be offered. Likewise, believers today may be painted as foolish or weak, their acts of devotion considered silly, and the final victory of Jesus scoffed at as a fairy tale. Nehemiah considered mockery a serious obstacle worthy of a strongly-worded prayer.

When a physical attack became the threat, Nehemiah both prayed again and posted guards. There is no conflict between trusting divine sovereignty while at the same time taking prudent precautions. Unless the Lord watched over the city of Jerusalem, the guards Nehemiah posted would stay awake in vain, but the Lord could use them to keep his people safe (Psalm 127:1). Jerusalem might be as surrounded by enemies as it was by mountains, but the Lord still surrounded his people and he would not abandon them (Psalm 125:2). Nehemiah kept directing the people's attention to their "great and awesome" God, a phrase echoed in Nehemiah 1:5 and Deuteronomy 7:21. He understood that true security lies in having God on your side (see 2 Chronicles 20:17).

The Bible gives many reasons why God allows our service to him to be difficult and seem unproductive. Among them:

- Hardships are evidence that we are God's children and that he is lovingly training us to trust him (Hebrews 12:3–11).
- Opposition from the world is a sign that we belong to Jesus, whose life followed the same pattern of suffering that leads through death to glory (John 15:18–20).
- Jesus is glorified in our weakness as we learn to trust him, and as we learn this trust we actually become stronger because we start working in *his* power rather than our own (2 Corinthians 12:7–10).
- The apparent foolishness and weakness of Jesus's kingdom is part of its glory and is judgment on those too proud to embrace it (1 Corinthians 1:17–21).
- Jesus's kingdom is not of this world, so its advances often are not visible to us and may look like setbacks even though he is accomplishing his purposes (John 18:33–37).

LESSON 8: THE JOY OF THE LORD

One noticeable feature of the assembly in Nehemiah 8 is the solemnity of the gathering and the respect shown for the Word of God. The people stand when Ezra brings out the scroll, and respond with a hearty *amen* ("May it be so!") after Ezra blesses

God, prostrating themselves in worship. Yet it is not so solemn that the reading of the scroll becomes cold and distant. The event is meant to affect hearts, and there is much room for both weeping and joy, as appropriate. Both Nehemiah and Ezra are present for the reading, combining the authority of the civil and religious leadership. Note, though, that Nehemiah is careful not to overstep. He leads the people, but does not presume to be a priest. In 10:1, he will be first among the princes to sign the written covenant, but at the dedication of the wall in 12:36 he follows the Levitical choir among the lay people, content to let Ezra lead the procession.

The key principles of gospel-believing worship services today include it being centered around God's Word, understood by the ordinary person, and guided by God's biblical directions for worship. Each of these is present in the assembly in Nehemiah. The reading of God's law is the focus, care is taken to make sure the people understand, and the feast is celebrated in careful compliance with biblical instructions (compare 8:13–18 with Leviticus 23:33–43). A gospel-believing worship service will also naturally be joyful about Jesus despite an appropriate sorrow over sin, and this too fits what we see in Nehemiah. The people's devotion to God's Word is impressive: four hours of attentive standing, care to understand, heartfelt receptiveness that extends even to weeping, and careful obedience afterwards to what they heard.

LESSON 9: TRUE REPENTANCE

If necessary, make sure your group understands the difference between *repentance* (the heart-level sorrow and resolve demonstrated in Nehemiah 9) and *penance*, a gospel-denying concept that includes suffering pain or performing difficult outward acts in order to appease God. Repentance is, along with faith, both an element in our initial conversion and an ongoing Christian lifestyle. As such, it is a gracious and life-giving work of the Holy Spirit in our hearts (Acts 11:18; 2 Timothy 2:25) and is the sort of resolve that never takes its eyes off Jesus—since repentance and faith are two sides of the same inner change. Penance, on the other hand, sidesteps the saving work of Jesus by attempting to add one's own suffering or righteousness to lessen the guilt of sin. We should reject penance but embrace repentance.

The sorrowful symbols used by the assembly in Nehemiah (fasting, sackcloth, dirt on the head, prostrating themselves before the Lord) were outward signs of inner grief, not legalistic acts of penance. True repentance in the heart will always show itself in the outer person, both in demeanor and in changed behavior, which is called the fruit of repentance (Luke 3:8–9).

Since true repentance cannot happen without true faith alongside of it, the Levites in Nehemiah were wise to emphasize God's redeeming acts along with sorrow over sin. God's kindness toward us is meant to lead us to repentance (Romans 2:4). The people did not just need to feel guilty; they needed to grieve over their sin before the God who saves from sin, believing in his saving acts and trusting him to save forever. This is the godly grief "that leads to salvation without regret, whereas worldly grief produces death" (2 Corinthians 7:10).

Formal and public promises to obey God are occasionally part of our spiritual lives too. For instance, many baptisms or church-joining ceremonies include such promises. God's commands deserve—in fact, demand—a heart response that desires to obey and resolves to follow that desire. Resolve itself is good (an element of repentance!), provided we realize that reliance on self-effort is foolhardy, and instead build our resolve on faith in Jesus. We must make our promises in a humble, trusting, prayerful way. It is Jesus, by the Spirit he gives us, who daily provides the strength to obey, and in whom we have full forgiveness when we fail.

DISCUSSION: As believers living between the two comings of Jesus, we are part of the era of fullest repentance in which repentance is proclaimed in Christ's name to all nations (Luke 24:47). We have advantages (and corresponding responsibilities) earlier believers did not know, and these motivate us to repent. We have seen in Jesus the tenderheartedness of God toward those who mourn over their sin (Luke 7:36–50). Through the cross and resurrection, we know more fully the stunning love, complete payment for sin, and eternal life that accompany repentance (Acts 3:18–21). We have the fullness of the Holy Spirit, who is in us to match our desires to his (Galatians 5:16–24). And we are on the cusp of the coming age, when the joy that heaven already has over repentant sinners will be ours forever in our Father's house (Luke 15:11–24). Remembering these truths for ourselves, and telling them when we share about Jesus, will help make any call to repentance also a proclamation of good news.

LESSON 10: LASTING REFORMATION

In most parts of the world today, the church faces challenges similar to those in Nehemiah's time. Especially when living amid a culture of unbelievers, there are temptations to accommodate worship to suit the culture's sensibilities, to bring the culture's idols into the church (perhaps without full awareness, or in seeming innocence: "we're only giving Tobiah one room, outside the sanctuary"), to neglect full support of ministries or missions, to disregard Sabbath/worship in favor of the culture's pursuits, or to overlook godliness in marriage/family life in favor of the sort of spouse and childrearing the culture values. Nehemiah teaches us to be vigilant against encroachments, which can come upon us quickly, and to hold to God's Word as our guide. Some separation from the world will be essential.

Nehemiah's enforcement methods may seem harsh, but it is important to understand what was at stake. Corruption from the surrounding cultures was a grave threat to proper worship, godly lifestyles, and children who would know the Lord. Seeing these dangers, Nehemiah combined traditional tactics of a civil governor with reminders from God's Word, recalling the strong warning against intermarriage in Deuteronomy 7:1–4 and the sad story of King Solomon from 1 Kings 11:1–10, where allowances for Ammonite and Moabite practices are highlighted as bringing about the kingdom's disasterous spiritual decline.

For more on the lineage, history, and worship practices of the Ammonites and Moabites, and on Ruth's acceptance into the assembly of Israel after renouncing her heritage, see Genesis 19:30–38; Leviticus 20:1–5; Numbers 22:1–6; Ruth 1:15–18; 4:10–17; 2 Chronicles 20:1–23; Zephaniah 2:8–11. During the wilderness period, Moab had attempted to put a curse on Israel, instead bringing the curse of exclusion from the Lord's assembly upon themselves in line with Genesis 12:3 and Deuteronomy 23:5. God will not spare those who oppose the ones he loves, yet his mercy is great toward any who repent.

mission
propelled by good news

At Serge we believe that mission begins through the gospel of Jesus Christ bringing God's grace into the lives of believers. This good news also sustains and empowers us to cross nations and cultures to bring the gospel of grace to those whom God is calling to himself.

As a cross-denominational, reformed sending agency with more than two hundred missionaries and twenty-five teams in five continents, we are always looking for people who are ready to take the next step in sharing Christ through:

- **Short-term Teams:** One- to two-week trips oriented around serving overseas ministries while equipping the local church for mission

- **Internships:** Eight-week to nine-month opportunities to learn about missions through serving with our overseas ministry teams

- **Apprenticeships:** Intensive twelve- to twenty-four-month training and ministry opportunities for those discerning their call to cross-cultural ministry

- **Career:** One- to five-year appointments designed to nurture you for a lifetime of ministry

 Grace at the Fray

Visit us online at: serge.org/mission

newgrowthpress.com